THE VIGIL

OTHER BOOKS BY WENDY M. WRIGHT

Silent Fire:
An Invitation to Western Mysticism
(With Walter Capps)

•

Bond of Perfection:
Jeanne de Chantal and Francois de Sales

•

Francis de sales and Jane de Chantal:
Letters of Spiritual Direction
(With Joseph F. Power OSFS & Peronne Marie Thebert VHM)

•

Sacred Dwelling:
A Spirituality of Family Life

•

Frances de Sales:
A Contemporary Reading

THE VIGIL

Keeping Watch in the Season of
Christ's Coming

Wendy M. Wright

Upper Room Books
Nashville

ISBN 0-8358-0661-8
Library of Congress Catalog Card Number: 91-67168
Printed in the United States of America.
First printing: August, 1992 (7).
Second printing: August, 1993 (5).

In gratitude to
CLARA, VIRGIL, DAVID, PAUL, & LARRY.

Each of whom,
for a season,
has kept close watch
with me.

CONTENTS

Acknowledgments

A BOOK DOES NOT START with its author nor end there. A community calls it forth and once an author has wrestled for a while with that call, the book goes back to the community and assumes a life of its own.

The editors, former and present, of Upper Room Books, notably Jill Reddig and Lynne Deming, first called this present book into being.

Dean Michael Proterra, SJ, and Father Thomas Shanahan, SJ, of Creighton University graciously arranged for release time for me during which I was able to complete the manuscript. A faculty development grant overseen by Dean Michael Lawler of Creighton's Graduate School provided funds for the word-processing of the book. Jackie Lynch of Omaha, Nebraska, saw the word-processing through from beginning to end.

Many others assisted me in wrestling with the call, especially Robert Benson of Upper Room Books, who was chief editor, attentive and intuitive listener, and the book's guardian angel. Father John Breck of St. Vladimir's Seminary, Father Dennis Hamm, SJ, of Creighton; my daughter, Emily Bergman; and my husband, Roger Bergman, likewise contributed valuable insights and information along the way, as did the staff of the reference department of the Reinart Memorial Library at Creighton.

Mostly the book comes from and returns to the many Christian communities with whom I have prayed and celebrated Advent and Christmas through the years: in particular, Hollywood First Presbyterian Church; All Saints by the Sea Episcopal Church and

Saint Barbara's Parish of Santa Barbara, California; St. Anne's Parish in Boston's Back Bay; the Weston School of Theology community in Cambridge, Massachusetts; and St. Cecilia's and Sacred Heart Parishes in Omaha, Nebraska.

To the Reader

THIS SMALL BOOK is an invitation offered to individuals and small groups who might wish to enter more prayerfully into the liturgical seasons of Advent and Christmas. Because of this, it follows the overarching rhythm of the Christian liturgical calendar. Its division into three larger sections, entitled WAITING, THE COMING, and LIVING THE SEASON, correspond to the periods of Advent, Christmas itself (Eve and Day), and the days following Christmas that culminate in Epiphany.

Each of these three larger sections is subdivided, also in correspondence to the liturgical movement. The Advent section is divided into four weeks, following the custom in the Western church of beginning observance four Sundays before Christmas itself. Its title, WAITING, reflects the pervasive mood of the season. I have taken the liberty of naming the four weeks according to four secondary themes that I feel characterize the whole of the waiting season: *Promise, Preparation, Rejoice,* and *Wonder.* While I have made use of the contemporary lectionary in preparing my thoughts on these themes, I have not chosen simply to follow the readings for the four Sundays. For one thing, these readings change from year to year according to the cycle of the calendar in which we find ourselves. Further, there are numerous weekday readings which flesh out the Sunday readings and enliven the picture they paint. Therefore, I have chosen to draw upon the vast wealth of Advent scripture and cull out from it the four themes mentioned above. Both contemporary commentaries and earlier, especially medieval, exegesis have informed my interpretations of these scriptures.

The second larger section, THE COMING, pertains to Christmas Eve and Day. It is subdivided into three parts, based upon the traditional medieval practice of celebrating three masses on the Feast of the Nativity. These commonly took place at midnight, dawn, and noon, mirroring what the medieval contemplative world referred to as the three births of God: of the Word eternally in the bosom of the Father, from the womb of Mary in the incarnation, and in the human soul. For each of these births I have chosen a theme which seems to me to spring naturally from the cumulative prayer of the Christian community: *Silence* (for midnight), *Poverty* (for dawn), and *God-with-Us* (for noontime).

The third section runs parallel to the days that follow Christmas (what the English call the Twelve Days of Christmas and which they used to celebrate by daily gift giving as the carol of that name reminds us) and ends with Epiphany. I have named it LIVING THE SEASON in the recognition that the liturgical calendar teaches us that Christmas does not end with the birth. Rather, the fruits of that feast must be consciously lived by us afterward, just as the birth of a child is but the beginning of a lifelong task of raising that child to adulthood. There are a variety of liturgical themes and experiences during this season. I have focused on three: *Dark* (reminiscent of both the Martyrdom of St. Stephen and the Feast of the Holy Innocents, the massacre of the male children around Bethlehem); *Peace* (recalling both the proclamation of the infancy narratives of peace on earth as well as the observance on the Roman calendar of New Year's as a feast of peace); and finally *Light* (reflecting the star imagery of the Western Feast of Epiphany itself and acknowledging the emphasis in the Eastern Orthodox churches on the reality of the light of the transfigured Christ).

The book is not intended to be a generic study guide for Advent and Christmas. Such commentaries have been done by those better equipped as scripture scholars or homilists than I. Instead, these reflections are frankly personal. Yet they are grounded, substantively I hope, in the wider theological and devotional life of the Christian community in both its historical and contemporary ecumenical dimensions. I have felt free to mix humorous anecdote, mystical exegesis, hymnody, family tales, poetry, visual imagery, and historical documentation in one narrative in the hope that, as readers keep vigil during the season of the Coming, they will find something here to accompany them on many levels and to deepen the experience of this most exquisite of all seasons.

THE BEGINNING

IT BEGINS IN THE BEGINNING. The vigil we keep has its true beginning long before any of us are born. It begins in the season before seasons, before the emergent cosmos exploded into being. It has its beginning in the heart of God. And so we must begin there as well.

The ancient desert dwellers of our early Christian communities tell us that the surest way into the heart of God is to be still. In being still we learn to be attentive to the vast and hidden stillness that permeates all things.

So I invite you to begin by becoming attentive to that stillness as well. Seek it first in your own home. Go at night into the darkened room of your sleeping child and breathe with the moist, quick risings of a child's breath. Rise in the thin light of a new day. Do not turn on the lamp or the television or the coffee maker, but stand by an east window and let the dawn's fingers creep up over the fingers of your own hand.

Listen next for stillness as you venture out of doors. Hear it in the splintering of fall leaves as you cross a grassy knoll between paths in the park. Find it in the first cape of snow draped over the eaves of your house.

Turn finally to your own heart. The same stillness is there as well. At the core, buried beneath the turbulence of emotions rubbed raw by life's labor, is the same stillness discovered in the slow-moving sap of an autumn tree. In that primordial stillness beats the heart of God.

There is correspondence between our hearts and God's. They have imprinted on them the same unimaginable hope, sealed with a promise. The hope is for fullness, for completion, for being one with each other. What that will look like is hidden from us. The end and fullness of all things is known only to God. But we have glimpses of it and those glimpses stagger us with their inexpressible beauty. We are tormented with teasing reminders by the restlessness of our desires, by the almost painful depth of our longings, by our ardent seeking for something more.

Our entire lives are a vigil, a keeping watch, for the fulfillment of this hope. All creation holds vigil with us, as it has done since the beginning. All generations before us and those that come after us will hold it as well.

But it is especially in this season of the church year, during Advent and Christmas, the season of the Coming, that we rise up on tiptoe to dance. We open our throats to sing and to proclaim this vigil that we keep.

As we do so we dip down into the ageless vigil being kept by the waters and grasses of the earth. We share the solemn watchfulness observed by granite and limestone. We enter the hearts of one another as, in stillness, we listen for the divine heartbeat.

We wait for the fullness. We watch for the completion of the promise. We vigil for the coming of the unimaginable fruition of the seed growing from the beginning in the heart of God.

WAITING

Come my Way, my Truth, my Life:
Such a Way, as gives us breath:
Such a Truth, as ends all strife:
Such a Life, as killeth death.

Come, my Light, my Feast, my Strength:
Such a Light, as shows a feast:
Such a Feast, as mends in length:
Such a Strength, as makes his guest.

Come, my Joy, my Love, my Heart:
Such a Joy, as none can move:
Such a Love, as none can part:
Such a Heart, as joys in love.[1]

GEORGE HERBERT
1593-1633

Promise

THERE IS SOMETHING MAGICAL ABOUT IT, especially as seen through a child's eyes. Every year in the first few days of December (and even earlier), the lights begin to go up. First, you see them in the stores or festooning the lamp posts in shopping districts. But, while these earliest lights are festive, they are usually too blatantly commercial, too much a Pavlovian prod that is meant to alert the holiday shopper to the need to get out and buy. And they are too opportunistically soon.

Rather, it is the lights that begin to dot the residential districts that weave the magical spell. In the single digit days of December my children daily point out new illuminations on our own block. "Look, the Watsons put up their big candle!" "Dan and Marty have their eaves lit up in a flashing triangle again!" Up and down the block the lights gradually appear. Draping low bushes or scaling the heights of tall trees, ringing an evergreen wreath or tracing a geometrical pattern around windows and doors, the lights are lit. There is the artful solemnity of the home with a dimly glowing "candle" in each window and the exuberant display of electric Santa's elves busy with their holiday preparations upon a neighbor's lawn.

As the season progresses, we take short excursions beyond our own neighborhood to view the displays of light. There are homey streets with scattered decorations—mainly multicolored strings that irradiate the chill darkness about them with red, green, white, and blue auras. Then there are the dazzling fantasies in the high mortgage district—cantilevered stars swinging from the tops of massive pines, dense tapestries of thousands of bulbs flashing on and off across the facade of colonial mansions, and whimsical trains of brilliance that seem to speed away on an invisible track laid on the circumference of well-manicured yards. My children and I love to watch the arrival of these seasonal lights. We love to drive through the frosty darkness of a

December evening and delight in the magical play of millions of bright sparkling bulbs. It is not only the sheer visual delight of the decorations that enamors us, it is the expectancy that they herald as well. We are teased into the spirit of a unique season of expectancy and hope, a season imaged by the emergence of a galaxy of lights from the dark of a winter night. We enter into the mystery of the Coming.

The Christian community has celebrated the extended Christmas season for centuries. The Feast of the Nativity of Jesus–Christmas itself–first emerged as a separate observance in the fourth century in the Western Church. It seems to have been fixed as an ecclesial observance on the twenty-fifth of December according to the usage of the Christian community in Rome. In the Eastern Christian (Orthodox) Church the Feast of Epiphany on January sixth was often associated with the Nativity. Some groups of Eastern Christians still celebrate Christmas on that day.

The liturgical origins of the before-Christmas preparation are discovered somewhat later in history. Scholars can point to the latter part of the sixth century for evidence of prayers and scriptural texts being written and selected to correspond to the Sundays of what we now call Advent (from the Latin *Adventus*–coming).

Advent was celebrated as a season of waiting, both for the Feast of Nativity, which is the church's liturgical window into the mystery of the incarnation, and for the Second Coming of Christ. In the West, Advent begins on the Sunday nearest to St. Andrew's Day (November 30). In the Eastern Church the season is longer, beginning mid-November. Because it was a period of preparation, Advent was historically observed as a time of solemnity and fasting. Vestiges of this earlier mood still linger in the penitential color of the vestments and the omission of celebratory parts of the service prescribed in liturgically oriented denominations.

For centuries Christians have turned to the passages in Scriptures that speak of the two comings of Christ. The two together are, of course, events in a single sacred history–the story of God's creation, redemption, and final judgment of the world. They are likewise two facets of the Christ event: the birth of the baby in Bethlehem, which was the moment when (to use the words of Eastern Orthodox writers) God became human in order that humans might participate in God; and the future coming of the risen Christ, who will sift and weigh the lives of all and usher in a transformed order of reality to fulfill the promises of God. Over the centuries Christians have woven the disparate threads of their personal and communal lives into the tapestry of this greater story. They have understood themselves to be the recipients of God's infinite and tender love through the gift of the incarnation, God becoming human. Likewise, they have looked, in both anticipation and trepidation, to the final coming when God's ultimate hope for creation itself will be realized.

The earliest Christians thought the Second Coming would be immediate, and they lived accordingly. Today, most of us live with a much less heightened sense of the last times. Most Christians operate with only a dim awareness of such apocalyptic imaginings and focus much more, liturgically and in their personal appropriations of faith, on the mystery of the first Coming–on "God-with-us." There are some striking exceptions to this among some long ago and some contemporary Christians who would focus so much upon a cataclysmic version of the Second Coming that the mystery of "God-with-us" and the indwelling of God's presence through the first coming seems to be forgotten.

During Advent, the season of the Coming, both Advents–past and future–are there to be celebrated. They are there to be reflected on, prayed over, wrestled with, and delighted in. For through the celebration of the seasons we come to know the ways of God. We begin our vigil. We enter into the expectancy, the joy, the wonder of the season of the Coming.

People of the Promise

Throughout the season of anticipation, the church raises up the voice of prophecy enshrined in the book of Isaiah. The liturgy resounds with the thrilling vision foretold there. It is a vision of the fullness of all things, of creation transfigured. The words paint a vivid and compelling picture that speaks to the deepest longings of our hearts.

Sometimes the vision of promise is cast in terms of a succulent banquet (which we Christians anticipate in our Eucharist or Communion). In our calorie and cholesterol conscious age, we might miss some of the wonder of the imagery if we did not first reflect on our own deepest hungers and be willing to relish being filled.

> On this mountain,
> Yahweh Sabaoth will prepare for all peoples,
> a banquet of rich food, a banquet of fine wines,
> of foods rich and juicy, of fine strained wines.[2]

The prophetic vision of the twenty-fifth and thirty-fifth chapters is one of the reversal of all sorrow and the vanquishing of all that tears at and weighs down the human heart.

> He will destroy death for ever.
> The Lord Yahweh will wipe away the tears
> from every cheek.[3]

> Then the eyes of the blind shall be opened,
> the ears of the deaf unsealed,
> then the lame will leap like a deer
> and the tongues of the dumb sing for joy. . . .[4]

Even creation itself, the whole of the cosmos, will turn itself inside out and be made anew.

> Let the desert and the dry lands be glad,
> let the wasteland rejoice and bloom. . . .
> let it burst into flower,
> let it rejoice and sing for joy.[5*]

And the final reconciliation of all things will occur.

> The wolf will live with the lamb,
> the panther lie down with the kid,
> calf, lion, and fat-stock beast together,
> with a little boy to lead them.
> The cow and the bear will graze,
> their young will lie down together.
> The lion will eat hay like the ox.
> The infant will play over the den of the adder;
> the baby will put his hand into the viper's lair.
> No hurt, no harm will be done
> on all my holy mountain,
> for the country will be full of the knowledge of Yahweh
> as the waters cover the sea.[6*]

Isaiah's vision is one of profound vitality, of a peace that is not simply the absence of conflict, but a peace that comes from holding together in love all the paradox of human experience—the kind of peace that is profoundly creative.

> They will hammer their swords into ploughshares
> and their spears into sickles.
> Nation will not lift sword against nation,
> no longer will they learn how to make war.[7*]

The voice of such prophecy can enflame our hearts. I wonder if too often we let these Advent words wash over us like pretty poetry, a faraway fantasy spun by someone long ago referring to something in a vague and shadowed future. But in fact these prophecies have their real root in the present. They have their origins in the structure of the human person. For daring to dream what is deepest in our collective longings is what makes us most human and fully alive.

Advent is a time in which we are invited to turn our attention to the fact that we are recipients of a promise. As a culture we seem to have little time for promises of the sort held out in Old Testament times, promises whose telling plunges us deep into the wideness and mercy of God. Instead, we attend to promises of a much more limited and transient nature: Buy this cosmetic and you will find beauty. Wear that brand of pantyhose and you will win love. Drive this model of car and you will achieve power. Attain this degree or that position and you will have fulfillment. Our media is filled with such promises. We even have a margarine that bears the name Promise. We purchase perfumes with labels like Joy, Knowing, and Dreams. To put it succinctly, as a culture we have co-opted our own ability to articulate and dream out of the most fundamental longings of our hearts.

To open ourselves to the possibility that there is a more radical, all-embracing promise than the ones offered by commercial enterprises eager to take our money and play on our restless longings in order that we might buy more is to begin to live the season of Advent.

What we all dream, what we all hope for is simple. We dream that the glimpses of the fullness of love that we sense occasionally in our lives, show us what we were created to become. When a young father takes his newborn daughter into his arms for the first time; when a mother eases the midnight fears of her frightened son, cradling him and recalling the intimacy of his infant mouth on her breast; when an estranged couple grope their way painfully back into love again; when a family makes a pilgrimage to the bedside of a dying loved one and finds itself bathed in the mystery of love; when a single woman comes to see her solitary dwelling not as a place of emptiness, but as a nest sheltered under the wing of God; when a community provides an environment for healing; when friends call us to remember our most authentic selves; when a strange and fearful person becomes for us the face of God; it is then that we begin to sense what we are intended to be, God's children, the children of promise.

How breathtakingly that promise is refracted for us in the Advent texts of Isaiah. This prophet's magnificent vision has always been understood in the Christian community to foretell a new age that is to be ushered in by a messianic saviour. And the earliest Christians interpreted these texts in retrospect to refer to Jesus of Nazareth, who was for them the promised one. Prophetic signs were seen to surround his coming and a mighty destiny to be his end.

> The Lord himself, therefore,
> will give you a sign.
> It is this: the maiden is with child
> and will soon give birth to a son
> whom she will call Immanuel.[8]

> For there is a child born for us,
> a son given to us
> and dominion is laid on his shoulders;
> and this is the name they give him:
> Wonder-Counsellor, Mighty-God,
> Eternal-Father, Prince-of-Peace.
> Wide is his dominion
> in a peace that has no end. . . . [9]

Generations of Christians have celebrated and allowed their hope to be enlivened by the messianic proclamation. They have prayed and preached and sung it. What would the pre-Christmas season be without singing along with or at least listening to Handel's *Messiah* with its contrapuntal setting of Isaiah's words? *For unto us a child is bo-o-o-o.* . . . Here the sopranos take off on a florid display of agility, and the basses, then the tenors and altos echo back. *Wonderful!* the chorus thunders. *Counselor!* they proclaim again. Then, emphatically,

The Might-y God! The combined voices descend down the scale, *The Everlasting Father,* and alight with calm repose upon the dominant tone, *The Prince of Peace.*

Music like this gives wings to Christian faith that the promise has its beginning in the birth of a child long ago who was the fulfillment of ancient Israel's prophecies. He was the one who was to give flesh to that startling, countercultural vision. In fact, Isaiah's very words as found in Isaiah 61 are echoed in the mouth of Jesus at the beginnings of his ministry by the evangelist in the Gospel of Luke.

> The spirit of the Lord Yahweh has been given to me
> for Yahweh has anointed me.
> He has sent me to bring good news to the poor,
> to bind up hearts that are broken;
> to proclaim liberty to captives,
> freedom to those in prison;
> to proclaim a year of favor from Yahweh,
> and a day of vengeance for our God,
> to comfort all who mourn.[10]

What this startling vision points to is a world transformed: a reality in which injustice and poverty are unknown, where the dispossessed and the vulnerable will be welcomed, where death itself and the inevitable sorrow and labor of life will be no more. This is what we long for, this is what we are promised, this is what has begun.

Believing the Promise

Promise is at the heart of the season of the Coming. Opening our hearts to the radical nature of the promise is the initial invitation of the liturgical moment in which we find ourselves. The further invitation is to believe. By belief I do not mean primarily intellectual assent, nor do I mean a sort of blind faith in something we are told we should assent to. To believe something (in a religious sense) is not simply to hold an opinion; it is to let that something sink down into the marrow of your bones and form the structure of your life. To believe something is to let its affirmation become the inhalation and exhalation of your life's breath. Belief does not exclude doubt or incredulity or intellectual curiosity, but belief is not exhausted in doubting or incredulity or curiosity. To believe something is to let it transform your life.

We know something of the wideness of God's promise through the longings of our own hearts and through moments of graced encounter with one another. But most of our moments are cluttered with concerns and busyness that tend to bury our hearts' longings. And most of our encounters with one another are fraught with the difficulties of communicating accurately or with the impossibility of seeing each other as anything but an obstacle to our own plans. It is in the church's liturgy and music of the Advent period that we become people who believe. The carols of the season especially help carry the submerged memory into consciousness.

Though the example seems a bit frivolous, an experience of my own of a number of years ago illustrates the point, I think. My husband and our then two children were living in the Boston area where he was attending graduate school. It was winter and I was in the first months of my third pregnancy, feeling desperately fatigued and continually nauseated. We were living on next to nothing in a tiny rent-controlled second floor apartment in the crush and noise of the city. Every week I dreaded grocery shopping. To bundle up two small children and take them out into the cold to hunt down the car we had parked somewhere on the overcrowded streets, to load them in and make the harrowing long drive through the treacherous "rotaries" that I never learned to negotiate without terror, to park in a snow banked icy lot and tiptoe my way (one child in tow, the other on hip) into the mammoth market where you had to procure a fingerprinted photo ID in order to cash a check, to negotiate (purse firmly under my arm) the aisles weighing the cost of every purchase I made, to wait with restless, sodden-diapered children in an endless checkout line only to discover that a mitten or hat had been lost along the way, to push an unwilling cart full of bags growing soggy in the falling drizzle out to the car, to load all this up only to make the terrorizing return trip, to double park outside our building, to haul the by now limp sacks up to the second floor while the children waited and whimpered in the car below, to spend at least one half hour dazedly searching for a parking spot, then to herd the by now miserable and complaining children out of the automobile for a five-block walk home through the gathering gloom and sleet to an apartment full of grocery sacks ominously tearing open at the seams: this I dreaded.

One Advent weekday during our Boston sojourn, when there genuinely was nothing left to eat in the house, the stock my husband had left on the shelves over the weekend being depleted, I decided to make the dreaded outing. I was in the full swing of Advent, with the palpable evidence of impending birth impressing itself upon my depleted consciousness. At our church, the music of the season had been liturgically correct, refraining from breaking into Christmas songs until the day itself, filling our hearts and minds instead with hymns of longing and anticipation. *O come, o come Emmanuel, and ransom captive Israel.* I certainly felt like I needed to be ransomed that day as I narrowly escaped colliding with a swiftly moving vehicle that had pulled in front of me from the left to make a right hand exit out of the free-for-all rotary. *Maranatha, come, Lord Jesus.* Bits of song floated randomly through my mind as I pulled into the parking lot clogged with exhaust-blackened snow. Inside the store, I lost track of any sense of the season, finding myself bathed in sweat in the overheated interior, struggling to find space in the shopping basket for our bulky jackets and mufflers. All the food lining the aisles looked particularly grim that day. I had just the previous week satisfied a bizarre craving for feta cheese, which left me sicker than before, and I found myself turning green at the heightened pungency of the sacks of bird seed and packages of raw liver that I passed. I wanted to cry, but my toddler was beating me to it because I was trying to extract from her a sheet of rumpled paper she had stuffed into her mouth. It was the grocery list, of course.

I had just entered the canned vegetable section and was trying to make out the handwriting on the wet shredded paper I had taken from her, and I had just reached my hand out to pick up a can of generic tomato paste, when I was suddenly stopped.

Joy to the world, the Lord is come! The percussive upbeat of the first notes of the carol bored a hole into my awareness as the supermarket Muzak was suddenly switched on.

Let earth receive her King! I stood there transfixed, with the tomato paste in my hand.

Let every heart prepare him room. The floodgates of my heart were flung open a vast and spacious wonderment filled me. *And heaven and nature sing, and heaven and nature sing. . . .*

Then I did start to cry, not out of frustration or fatigue, but out of a sense of the vividness of the promise, out of a sense of the magnificence of God's mercy and God's desire for us. God's children, we are *God's* children.

I picked up my fretful daughter and held her, clutching the tomato paste in my free hand. And I sang into her wet cheek, *And heaven and heaven and nature sing!*

In retrospect I have felt as though that moment in the Boston supermarket was the beginning of my belief in the promise.

Blessed is the One Who Believes

During this liturgical season we often hear the infancy narratives proclaimed. Those wonderful, tender passages we memorized as children are woven into our hearts as we listen to our own little ones, robed in burlap with shepherds' staves or haloed with glittering cardboard, declare: "In those days a decree went out from Caesar Augustus that the whole world should be enrolled" (Luke 2:1).

The infancy narratives are one of the many windows on the season that help us see into the mystery held close in the heart of God.[11] We have a bit of a tendency, remnants I think of our childhood faiths coupled with our modern adult propensity to literalism, to either reduce the infancy narratives to supposedly factual accounts or dismiss them as charming, naive tales. They are, in fact, not so much biographical information on the origin and birth of Jesus (about which we know virtually nothing) as rich perspectives on the mystery of divine and human life. They are narrative accounts compiled by the early Christian community which speak to the *meaning* of the Christ event. They paint word pictures and preserve for us their own readings, their own windows upon those truths. And, in the life of the community, the infancy narratives do not end with the text of scripture. Patristic and medieval scriptural exegesis, artistic renderings of the Gospels (visual, literary, musical, or architectural), theological insights and prayers, contemplative and visionary expressions and devotional practices that have been articulated over the centuries, historical critical methods of scripture analysis, and our own individual interpretation and integration of the word all serve to refract and give us access to their inexhaustible truth.

The infancy narrative of the Gospel of Luke especially speaks of the birth of Jesus as the fulfillment of promise. Laced throughout the Lucan text are evocative illusions to Isaiah's prophecies. The wondrous, even astonishing, culmination of the eschatological hope articulated by the Hebrew prophet is written in every phrase. Over the years, one image from that narrative has especially spoken to me. It is an image used frequently in both the Old and New Testaments:

barrenness becoming fruitful. We hear it in vegetative language in Isaiah: the desert shall blossom, the wilderness will become a place of springs. But in Luke the barrenness is found in the body of a woman. The motif is not unique in biblical literature. It recalls such Hebrew mothers as Sarah (Genesis 15:3, 16), Rebekah (Genesis 25:21), and Rachel (Genesis 29:31), but it has special significance when used, as it is in Luke, to accompany the mystery of the incarnation.

Elizabeth, wife of Zechariah, the text tells us, was advanced in years and barren. In a heavenly vision her husband received notice that they would conceive and bear a late-in-life child. It was during an Advent season several years ago that I came to appreciate this woman. For years I had been much focused on the figure of young Mary in the Advent season. Then, sometime after the birth of our last child, Elizabeth began to come into my prayer. As astonishing as Mary's pregnancy might have been, announced as it was by an angelic messenger and all, Elizabeth's conceiving began to seem even more remarkable. I found myself imaging the younger of the two women as moist and green, a fresh bud ripening in the sun. Extraordinary as her pregnancy was, her fruitfulness was in season. She was (and has been sung as such in Marian devotion for ages) a symbol of the fertility of the creation itself, ready to receive God. But Elizabeth came to me not as running streams and greening shoots, but as the dry, gray sand of the desert. She was parched creation grown unable to give new life. I began to wonder about *her* waiting. What must it have been like to wait long beyond the time when hope could reasonably be summoned? In Israel childlessness was a terrible thing, an occasion for mourning and shame. Whatever we think of having children or not having children in our contemporary world, for this woman, in her historical moment, barrenness defined her social identity. Her experience was one of promise *un*fulfilled.

Yet she must have been a woman whose grasp of the promise was so deep that she could continue to wait and to be open to the experience of radical surprise long after such waiting and such openness made any sense. She has become for me a true symbol of one who is blessed because she believed that the promises made would be fulfilled. She is a sign of all in our lives that to all appearances has ceased to be capable of giving life. She is a triumphant image of the capacity to receive God. She is a sign of new life in the face of present-day political and ecological realities that threaten our belief that such a promise of reality made new can truly be realized.

Elizabeth, the barren woman of advanced years, invites us into a waiting for the promise that becomes belief. She is one whose being has been recreated from the inside out when it was impossible. She has known in her flesh the prophecy of Isaiah 65 and 66. She beckons us into the vigil for the promise begun in the babe at Bethlehem whose fulfillment still remains hidden in the heart of God.

> I am going to create new heavens and a new earth. . . .
> I shall be joyful in Jerusalem
> and I shall rejoice in my people.
> No more will the sound of weeping be heard there,
> or the sound of a shriek;
> never again will there be an infant there
>   who lives only a few days
> nor an old man who does not run his full course. . . .
> Rejoice with Jerusalem,
> be glad for her, all you who love her![12]

Preparation

ADVENT IS A WONDERFUL TIME TO BE PREGNANT. All three of my pregnancies have fallen in some part during that magical season, heightening both the experience of the liturgy and the experience of carrying a child. For of all types of waiting, the waiting of pregnancy is most like the waiting that we do during Advent. The waiting of pregnancy is like the waiting we do for God. We carry hidden within ourselves new life. Not simply in the sense of renewal, but new life particularized, personalized, and uniquely enfleshed. We wait with unimaginable longing to see the face of the one we know to be already with us. Like an unborn child, the life of God grows unseen yet profoundly felt. Insistently pushing and prodding us, enlarging the contours of our lives and our hearts, as intimate to us as our own breathing, yet utterly other, the divine presence waits to be born.

With my first child, the correspondence of the liturgical mood with the shape of my own body and heart was the most marked. According to the physician's calculations I was due December 17, and by the checkup the first week of December, I was being kidded about not wanting to miss any Christmas holiday cheer through the inconvenience of having a baby. "Don't be surprised if it's later than the due date," I was told. And I was, in my cleverness, going to outwit the anxious anticipation of the last weeks by simply settling on the idea that this child wanted to be born on Christmas Day itself or during the follow-up season. I was content to wait.

I was cantoring at our parish Sunday celebration, and my assignment for the first week of Advent that year was to intone a proclamation based on the fifth chapter of Paul's letter to the Thessalonians.

> About times and dates, brothers, there is no need to write to you
> for you are well aware in any case that the Day of the Lord will

come like a thief at night. It is when people are saying, 'How quiet and peaceful it is,' that sudden destruction comes upon them, as suddenly as labor pains come on a pregnant woman; and there is no escape.

. . . . so we should not go on sleeping, as everyone else does, but stay wide awake and sober.[13*]

Two days later, completely unexpectedly, the little prophecy I had sung the preceding Sunday came true. Our daughter was born on Tuesday, December 6, without so much as a flicker of warning. It was not an easy birth. In my nonchalance I had neglected to marshal the inner energies that I would need for this most profound rite of passage. The Advent caught me groping for a psychic mooring on which to anchor myself in the turbulent seas of childbirth. It was a striking lesson in the truth that we do not control or know the ultimate order of things. It is best, therefore, to be alert and watchful. And to prepare.

"Prepare!" was the message of the promised child of Elizabeth, wife of Zechariah. The infancy narratives in Luke tell us that the child's father was struck dumb because he doubted an angelic message telling him of his child to be and that his tongue was only loosened again after he had bestowed on his son the name of John. This cousin of Jesus was to be the herald of the Messiah. Tradition has depicted John as a fiery ascetic emerging from a desert solitude to trumpet forth the words of Isaiah.

> A voice cries in the wilderness:
> Prepare a way for the Lord,
> make his paths straight.
> Every valley will be filled in,
> and every mountain and hill be laid low,
> winding ways will be straightened
> and rough roads made smooth.
> And all mankind shall see the salvation of God.[14]

The cry of John the Baptist, "Prepare!" echoes throughout the readings of the Advent season. He is one who announces the Coming, wondrous new age to be ushered in through Jesus. He is also one who warns: To be awake and watchful is not necessarily a simple matter; one must prepare.

Getting Ready

For most Americans, the weeks before Christmas are the yearly time par excellence for getting ready. Some of that readying is linked to our frantic consumer ethos. We make holiday gift lists, fight traffic congestion in shopping mall parking lots, endure endless checkout lines, press through crowds of shoppers in tinsel decorated business districts, overspend, overeat, over drink, over-party, overextend ourselves addressing greeting cards to persons we neglect the rest of the year, and generally wind ourselves up to anxious frazzles.

But there are other kinds of getting ready that go on among us. Beyond the commercial exchange of merchandise that has come to characterize the American pre-Christmas season is the reality that this tends to be a family time of year. There are innumerable family and community rituals of readiness that are enacted, strengthening bonds between loved ones of every shape and kind.

Rituals encase memories. They link the past and present. They choreograph the dance of intimacy that families and friends perform. They give us access to one another. They enable us to move together gracefully through times of transition. Sometimes rituals facilitate growth. Sometimes they express the breaches gaping between us. But always, rituals have power.

There is nothing so deeply rooted in the Advent memories of people as family rituals of preparation. I can still feel the warmth of a California December day through the pane glass window as I pressed my nose against it and peered out of the hundreds of peepholes created by the stenciled, flocked snowflakes, seeing through the artificial winter prism the brilliant colors of sun drenched flowers.

I remember too the special tree-buying ritual my father and I recreated with solemn precision each year. We would head out to a tree lot or, preferably, to the freight yards downtown where carloads of freshly cut firs and scotch pines lay in fragrant piles waiting in the Southern California sun to be purchased. We would start the search for the perfect tree. Long and hard we would hunt, surveying one tree after another with professional eyes only to move on, declaring "No, no, no–this is not *the* one." After seemingly endless circumambulation of innumerable clusters of trees, we would both suddenly shout, at the same instant, "This is it! We found it!" And we would triumphantly bring our tree back home. It was always the loveliest Christmas tree we had ever had.

Then there were the new rituals that developed as our extended family grew. There was the tree trimming party at my cousin Judy's, where her three small children and their preschool friends were the major actors in a delightful drama. Their bare tree, always a mammoth, long and thickly needled affair that filled half the living room, was the stage upon which this drama was played out. Several other moms had helped the children glue, cut, glitter, and staple a potpourri of paper, styrofoam and yarn decorations. "Be creative" was the one guideline, so there were artifacts of amazing variety: soggy paper chains dotted with caramel corn, truncated snowmen with spiraled pipe cleaners on their heads, snowflakes the size of jumbo pizzas. The culmination of the party came with the decoration of the tree. Everyone dashed for the empty branches at once, placing their new creations, as well as salvaged treasures from previous years, upon waiting limbs. Because everyone doing the trimming was under four feet tall, the lower branches of the tree were soon sagging, foil and tissue scrambled in chaotic array. The top half of the tree was left pristine in its nakedness. And so it remained throughout the season, honoring the efforts of the small trimmers who had come to decorate the tree.

Many families have food preparation rituals that mark the getting ready season. Holiday breads and their unique nostalgic fragrances trigger memories of a grandmother's kitchen. Fancy cookies link us with our ethnic roots—the anise seed scents of *springerle* recall German Christmas preparation; in Eastern Orthodox families the makings of *zalabee* or *awan* (homemade doughnuts) are part of the celebration of Epiphany; *marrons glaces* or candied chestnuts are special Mexican Christmas treats; *bûche de Noël* is an elegant French holiday confection. Faded *wassail* recipes come out of files connecting us through the tastes of the season with our jolly toasting English ancestors.

Other ethnic customs decorate the season. The tradition of *Las Posadas* has filtered from Mexico into many communities. For nine days preceding Christmas Eve, Mexican villagers customarily file through the streets at night, carrying candles and statues of Joseph and the pregnant Mary riding on a donkey. They sing a plaintive refrain recalling the holy couple's search for shelter. On each night they stop at a designated dwelling. "No, no shelter, no *posada,*" they are told. The procession continues each night until finally the doors of a dwelling are opened. "Welcome Joseph! Welcome Mary! Welcome the Christ child into our hearts." The *posada* ends with a celebration and the breaking of the *piñata,* the bright paper-covered earthenware jar filled with candies and toys.

Some of us observe the Advent feasts of Saint Nicholas and Saint Lucy imported by Germanic and Scandinavian Christians. On the eve of December 6, many European children put out their shoes to be filled by St. Nicholas who, according to legend, was an early Christian bishop who saved three impoverished young women from a life of forced prostitution by secretly supplying them with bags of gold for their dowries. Nicholas is thus the giver of secret gifts. Scandinavian families continue to celebrate Lucy's Feast on December 13 by having the youngest girl in the family costume herself in white and deck her hair with a crown of candles. Early in the morning she brings cakes baked specially for the feast to her family in bed. The crown of lights and the story of Lucy's martyrdom–during the Diocletian persecutions, in the course of which she lost her eyesight–symbolize the coming dawning of the light of Christ.

Similarly, there are family rituals that link the domestic church (the home) with the gathered church community. Advent calendars are a favorite of ours. Colorful panoramas of snow-flecked forest glens inhabited by cherubic angels, graceful line drawings of the cave in the Judean desert into which the long robed shepherds peer, a circle of pink-cheeked children kneeling in tender adoration around a tiny crib–these form the background out from which one daily presses tiny paper windows to discover a Bible verse or cunning pictured toy.

Then there is the Advent wreath with its four stately candles. Their nightly lighting marks off the days of anticipation, drawing us closer and closer into the vortex of the holiday we long to enjoy. Other families have their own customs: wreaths, holly, special prayers or readings for the Advent days, stockings, yule logs, constructing ornaments, putting out a Nativity set. We hide the baby Jesus until Christmas Eve when we place him in the manger. My son has added his own ritual element by placing the wise men and their camels on the window ledges at the far edge of the room and moving them one step closer toward the stable each day. The preparations are as varied as those who engage in them. What they express in common is the primal human instinct to ritualize our deepest apprehensions and hopes, in this case, our sense of the coming of God into our lives.

Repent

In the not so long ago past, Advent was observed in the church's liturgy much as Lent still is today. The preferred liturgical color of the season was purple, symbolic of penance, and fasting and solemnity were part and parcel of the season of the Coming. As a church we have moved away from this aspect of the season, but the scriptures still proclaim to us that preparation involves thoughtful reflection and readjustments in the priorities of our lives.

The arresting message of John the Baptist, as recorded by Luke, rings out from pulpits all over the world at this time of year.

> He said, therefore, to the crowds who came to be baptised by him, 'Brood of vipers, who warned you to flee from the coming retribution? Produce fruit in keeping with repentance, and do not start telling yourselves, "We have Abraham as our father," because, I tell you, God can raise children for Abraham from these stones. Yes, even now the ax is being laid to the root of the trees, so that any tree failing to produce good fruit will be cut down and thrown on the fire.
>
> '. . . I baptise you with water, but someone is coming, who is more powerful than me, and I am not fit to undo the strap of his sandals; he will baptise you with the Holy Spirit and fire. His winnowing-fan is in his hand, to clear his threshing-floor and to gather the wheat into his barn; but the chaff he will burn in a fire that will never go out.[15]*

This is a sobering earful for the busy holiday shopper focused on finding just the right gift for everyone, the choir director consumed with concern for the successful fundraising outcome of the school Christmas concert, or the office worker fretful about finding the perfect dress to wear to the upcoming office party.

Repent. What does this mean? It means, first, stopping for a while. It means that *not* doing must also be part of our preparation. It means we must take some time and slow down. We must look closely at our lives as they are, marking where they are God-directed or not.

Then we must begin to make the slow and ever-necessary turning around to place our feet firmly on the straight path that will lead us into the arms of our waiting God.

The scriptural imagery of the season is clear. God is coming to us. But in order for that truly to happen, we must go as well to God. The highway runs in two directions. The invitation is for the divine and human to meet halfway. At that meeting place the deep mystery of the season comes into being.

Looking closely at our lives is not as simple as it might seem. For I think we often assume we know what it is to be God-directed even before we stop and look. We assume that being a good Christian looks a certain way. Some of us too quickly assume that repentance is about actions—not yelling at our kids or serving on yet another church committee. Others of us may assume that it is about attitudes—letting go of resentment toward a bossy sibling or marshaling the discipline to embark on a regimen of prayer. Repentance has, in fact, both outer and inner dimensions and involves our willingness to reflect upon those actions and attitudes that habitually shape our lives.

It is all too easy for us to try to live out stereotypes of a Godly life. In our churches, we see prayerful, committed people that we admire, and so we want to be like them (or what we think they are). Or we take to heart what some spiritual author has said about the Christian life and its pitfalls, and so we want to direct our paths to avoid falling in the designated traps. But those traps may or may not be the ones we should be wary of, and those admirable church elders may or may not be living lives we are personally called to by God.

There is no such thing as generic holiness, no such abstract reality as the Christian life. There is only a concrete life that has intersected with the power of the Word and the transformative action of grace. The real mystery of our incarnated faith is that the divine comes to live in our particularity, to change us, yes, but always within the confines of our specificity–our own stories, our own limitations, our own needs, our own desires. Thus, to begin the process of making straight the paths, we must be rooted in our own truths.

What personally constitutes a God-directed life, either inner or outer, is not necessarily self-evident. Each of us must make an individual discernment, allowing the words of scripture, the witness of our faith communities, and our own diligent consciences to tease us into risky self-disclosure. What our looking reveals may surprise us.

Christian commentators have for centuries been attempting, within the contexts of their own cultural horizons, to describe the repentance with which the Baptist challenges us. Three of the Advent sermons delivered in 1620 by Francis de Sales, author of the widely read inspirational book, *Introduction to the Devout Life,* have been preserved for us. The sermons, from the second, third, and fourth weeks, each deal with the figure of the camel-hair-clad, locust-eating John. The last Sunday's talk addresses repentance directly. Francis de Sales expands on the gospel text by focusing on the interior qualities of our seasonal self-reflection.

> St. John gives some particulars in today's Gospel. Make straight the way of the Lord, fill up the valleys, lower the mountains and hills. They, as well as the ditches and valleys, trouble travelers. Make straight the paths. Those that twist and turn fatigue the pilgrim greatly. Our life too contains many hills, valleys and tortuous ways which can be put right only by penitence. Penitence fills up the valleys, lays low the mountains, makes straight and smoothes the ways. Do penance, says St. John; lower those mountains of pride, fill up those valleys, those ditches of lukewarmness and tepidity.
>
> The valleys which the glorious St. John wants us to fill up are none other than fear which, when it is excessive leads to discouragement at the sight of our sins. Fill up the valleys; that is, fill your heart with confidence and hope because salvation is near at hand [Lk. 21:28; Rom. 13:11]. The sight of our great faults brings with it a certain horror and shock, a certain fear and

terror which unnerves the heart and often leads it to discouragement. These are the ditches and valleys that must be filled up for Our Lord's coming.[16]

The Counter-reformation bishop names some of the inner habits that clutter the highways of our hearts and keep them from being paths that can lead us home to God. He asks the questions: Have we loved well or not? How have we refused or neglected the law of love? What are the overarching motions of our hearts that bar us from responding to the two great commandments of love of God and neighbor? Francis de Sales singles out pride, lukewarmness, fear, and discouragement as inner dispositions needing our attention at this time of year.

But there are other heart habits that the Christian tradition does not so clearly name for us that merit our Advent consideration. There may be other ways of coming to the season that tradition has not yet articulated for us. And I am not sure that the modern world even understands the true spirit of repentance to which that traditions tries to direct us. Repentance is not necessarily the gloomy and self-loathing practice it is sometimes made out to be. To repent is not to be confirmed in what that little voice within keeps whispering: that you are no good, that everything bad that happens to you is your own fault, that if only others knew what you were really like, they would cease to care for or be interested in you. No. True repentance begins with the felt knowledge that we are loved by God. We are children of God. If we cannot find ourselves there then perhaps our preparation might consist of the prayer that we might know ourselves as beloved, that the divine lover might reach down into our self-hatred, created perhaps by the lovelessness we learned as children or through our culture, and touch us.

Even if we have a glimpse of the way God loves us, the invitation of Advent is to look beyond stereotypes of the repentant or the perfect person to discern there the freedom of the children of God to which we are all called. Then we must take a fresh look at what keeps each of us, uniquely, from that freedom. For women, I think, the task is made subtly difficult because the Christian tradition does not always define "sin" in ways that resonate with women's experience. Whereas tradition would hold up pride and the lust to power as treacherous pitfalls in the quest for virtue, many women might be seen to be unfree (sinful) in their lack of self-definition, in their tendency to want to please others at the expense of self-integrity, in their enabling or codependent behavior. To define a healthy self that can be in a mutual relationship, to be courageous enough to reverence self even though not everyone will approve, to confront abusive or destructive patterns of interaction—these are not signs of pride or the desire for power. They are signs of knowing one's belovedness. What one repents of in these instances must be defined in a fresh way, as must the act of repentance itself. Repentance consists not so much in flagellating ourselves over our "failures" as in courageously and painstakingly reorienting our priorities, unlearning old patterns, turning our faces, like the sunflower, toward the dawning of the light of God.

But our seasonal repentance is not only inner, it is outer and communal as well. The majestic promises of Isaiah toward which we yearn are promises of a world renewed, not merely the renewal of individual hearts. The Hebrew prophet sings eloquently of the inclusion of the poor and marginalized and the institution of God's justice on earth.

> He shall judge the poor with justice
> and defend the humble in the land with equity;
> his mouth shall be a rod to strike down the ruthless,
> and with a word he shall slay the wicked.
> Round his waist he shall wear the belt of justice,
> and good faith shall be the girdle around his body.[17] (KJV)

The divine justice personified here is not the forensic justice we associate with law enforcement, but the distributive justice preached by the Baptist himself. How do we repent? John, as portrayed in Luke's Gospel, makes his answer clear.

> When all the people asked him, 'What must we do, then?' He answered, 'If anyone has two tunics he must share with the man who has none, and the one with something to eat must do the same.' There were tax collectors too who came for baptism, and these said to him, 'Teacher, what should we do?' He said to them, 'Exact no more than your rate.' Some soldiers asked him in their turn, 'And what is it that we should do?' He said to them, 'No intimidation! No extortion! Be content with your pay!'[18]

His answer exposes a different face of repentance than does the answer given by Francis de Sales. One speaks primarily of inner dispositions, the other of outer communal actions. Both give us important insights into the experience and practice of repentance in the season of the coming. The Baptist admonishes us: Whoever has two cloaks should share with the person who has none. Whoever has food should do likewise. Do not take more than your share. Do not oppress others. The message is clear.

In many ways contemporary Christians of all denominations do try good-heartedly to respond to the challenge of divine justice during the Advent season. Schools and congregations collect canned goods for Christmas baskets. Charitable organizations mount campaigns to collect toys for needy or ailing children. Businesses sponsor seasonal appeals for tax deductible groups that provide goods and services to the poor. Posters show radiant tots with their legs sustained in braces purchased by the goodwill of numerous donors. Shoppers drop their loose change into the buckets of Salvation Army bell ringers. Giving is part of the preparation for the season.

But the challenge cuts deeper than that. And this is where we, as a nation and as Christians within that nation, tend to balk. For all our generous giving to the poor, we often hesitate to inquire into the political, social, and economic conditions that create and sustain poverty. Or we relieve ourselves of the necessity for inquiring by assuming that the poor are lazy or morally inferior or in some way choose their lot. We tend to extend this kind of non-inquiring attitude to our global community. While we Americans are notable for the largesse of our emergency foreign aid, we seem content politely to ignore the massive discrepancies between the consumption of wealth and energy by those of us who are a small fragment of the world population and the lack of such resources in most other nations in the world.

The giving called for as part of our Advent repentance, our orienting our lives in the direction of the straight path, is more than charity. We are called to examine our collective life-style and adjust it so that, as the Baptist admonishes, we will not have excess food and clothing when others go without; we will not use more than our share; we will not live off the interest gained from others' impoverishment. The implications of such a challenge are immense.

Yet, let us remember that we are not asked to solve all these problems by ourselves overnight but simply to let our hearts be opened so that we might come to know what we are able to do. There is a Haitian proverb that says, "What the eye doesn't see doesn't move the heart." Advent is the liturgical time when we long to see. *O, come, O come, Emmanuel,* we sing. Let us see your face.

The face of the longed-for God is already all around us in the faces of those who, in their poverty, hunger, and desperation, truly live in hope of the fulfillment of the prophet's promise. Perhaps some of our outer preparation this season might be to let our hearts be moved by letting our eyes see. Might our giving go beyond writing out a check, purchasing a few extra canned goods, or sorting through used toys? Might we begin again quite literally the ancient Christian practice of the corporeal works of mercy: feeding the hungry, giving drink to the thirsty, welcoming the stranger, clothing the naked, tending the ill, visiting the prisoner, and burying the dead? Might we let our hearts be opened to spend time with and truly see these, the least among us?

We have a small but, for us, significant family ritual that is part of our vigil during this season. Every Christmas we go with several other people to one of the local homeless shelters and sing Christmas carols. We do not go to perform or spread seasonal cheer but to raise our voices together with our often forgotten brothers and sisters in wonder at the mystery God gives to us each year. It is there, among people whose childhood dreams have vanished, whose lives seem empty of promise, that the words of the carols the rest of us sing so glibly become clear. In that setting, songs of snowmen and Christmas wish lists and hearty good cheer ring hollow. But the carols of the mystery take on luminous meaning. It is for all of us, and especially these, that the Coming takes place. These are the ones the Baptist admonishes us to remember as we prepare the way for the Lord.

There is one gentleman from several Christmases ago whom I will never forget. Our little choir had been singing long enough in the smoke-filled, noisy shelter to be ready to wind up our sing-a-long. Then a disheveled man of about fifty in a soiled jacket, whose perceptions of things, due either to ill health or some chemical substance, seemed doubtful, asked me to sing his favorite Christmas song. It was "O Holy Night" he said; would I do it with him? I agreed and began. The crowded room gradually grew silent as he and I raised up our two voices together. He leaned on the edge of a tattered sofa about three feet from me, his eyes closed, the tired creases of his street-weary face softening as he intoned. We moved deeper into the melody, exploring the accelerated tempo and rising pitch that evoked the Christmas miracle.

> *Long lay the world in sin and error pining,*
> *'til he appeared and the soul felt its worth.*
> *A thrill of hope, the weary world rejoices*
> *as yonder breaks a new and glorious morn!*

As he strained his gravelly voice to give wings to the song's words, his face shone and tears fell gently from his lowered eyes. I knew, at that moment, that his longing and mine were one, and that the burning for the fulfillment of the promise that I felt was not only mine, it is etched on the human heart. It is our shared longing, our same desire, our common life.

The promises we anticipate during Advent are promises that the world as we know it will be overturned. "Prepare the way!" we are exhorted. "Make straight his paths." We are not only to await the Coming in joyful anticipation, we are to participate in it as well. We are called to inner and outer repentance, to an acknowledgment of the ways we have or have not smoothed the rough ways for the arrival of our God. Our repentance is but the lived recognition that we yearn for the overturning of things as they are and joyously cooperate in the reversal of the reign of death and sorrow that at present envelop us, as individuals, as nations, and as the global community.

The seventh chapter of the Gospel of Luke tells of John the Baptist sending several disciples to Jesus to ask him if indeed he is the promised one to come. In reply, Jesus points to the reversal dynamic inherent in the reign of God, which he inaugurates by healing many. He turns to the Baptist's followers and says:

> 'Go back and tell John what you have seen and heard: the blind
> see again, the lame walk, lepers are cleansed, and the deaf hear,
> the dead are raised, the Good news is proclaimed to the poor.' [19]

Might our preparations, our repentance, begin to bring about such reversals in ourselves and in our world? In doing so, we dip down into the soul of that great and cosmic vigil being kept from the beginning of time. For all of creation is embarked on that slow journey homeward to its final consummation. And humankind, as *homo adorans*, of all the creatures the one designed to worship and adore, is called to consciously chart and pilot that movement home.

Rejoice

THE VIGIL WOULD NOT SEEM LIKE IT HAD BEGUN in our house without the visual reminder of the Advent wreath. The day (or sometimes late the night) before the first Sunday, one or another of our children can be found scrounging around the neighborhood, hunting for an evergreen branch of classic scent and proportions, which we will snip and shape to form a fresh green halo to circle our four candles. Other families I know have handsome ceramic or glass wreaths, which they store neatly away in boxes from year to year. But I like the look and aroma of the newly cut boughs, even though by the end of the season the needles are usually shedding and brown at the tips.

Because the Advent season often catches me unaware, having had my attention recently submerged in the festivities surrounding Thanksgiving, I generally do not have the right candles on hand, and it would not seem like Advent if the traditional three purple tapers and one rose taper were not displayed. So there is a hurried trip to the church goods shop across town or, if that is not feasible, a frantic hunt at the local all-purpose store for candles whose colors will approximate the liturgically correct hues. The one rose colored candle is my favorite; its lighting on the third Sunday places it deeply within the penitential rhythm symbolized by the purple tapers of the other three Sundays that surround it.

The mood of this third Sunday contrasts strikingly with the others. In the old Roman rite it was always referred to as Gaudete Sunday, for the first word proclaimed (in Latin) at the Introit of the Mass—*Gaudete!* Rejoice! The joyous sentiment is echoed in Paul's letter to the Philippians, which is often read on this third Sunday.

> Always be joyful, then, in the Lord; I repeat, be joyful. Let your good sense be obvious to everybody. The Lord is near. Never

worry about anything; but tell God all your desires of every kind in prayer and petition shot through with gratitude, and the peace of God which is beyond our understanding, will guard your hearts and your thoughts in Christ Jesus.[20]*

Advent is not only a time of promise and preparation, it is a time to rejoice. The rejoicing we do is in great part a celebration of the initial fulfillment of the promise made; it is a living into the unspeakable mystery that has already occurred and which is at the heart of the season. The mystery is this: that God is born. Not only does this mystery speak to us of the inexpressible compassion of our God, who has entered intimately into history in order to participate fully in all that is most human, but it recalls for us that creation itself, especially the human person, has become the sacred locus of the encounter of the finite and the infinite. It is in the womb of the world that the radical promise of a new creation has been conceived, gestated, and born.

Magnificat

Of all the canticles preserved for us in the Christian scriptures over the centuries perhaps the most beloved has been the Magnificat found in the Gospel of Luke, the exquisite hymn of rejoicing sung by Mary, the young woman pregnant with her first child, in the presence of her cousin Elizabeth. Mary, after being visited by an angel of God who announces that she will soon bear a son, goes to Judah on her own visitation to her older cousin, whose shameful barrenness has now been taken away. The two women meet and the child in Elizabeth's womb is said to leap for joy at the approach of the fulfillment of the promise hidden beneath the folds of Mary's gown. Then Luke's Gospel places these words of rejoicing in the young mother's mouth:

> 'My soul proclaims the greatness of the Lord
> and my spirit exults in God my Savior;

Because he has looked upon his lowly handmaid.
Yes, from this day forward all generations
   will call me blessed,
for the Almighty has done great things for me.
Holy is his name,
and his mercy reaches from age to age
   for those who fear him.
He has shown the power of his arm,
he has routed the proud of heart.
He has pulled down princes from their thrones
   and exalted the lowly.
The hungry he has filled with good things,
   the rich sent empty away.
He has come to the help of Israel his servant,
   mindful of his mercy–
according to the promise he made to our ancestors–
of his mercy to Abraham and his descendants
    for ever.' [21]

The canticle is dense with layers of meaning that centuries of Christian exegetes and preachers have uncovered for us. But first and foremost, this is a song of rejoicing. It is the song of a young woman shyly placing one hand upon a swelling belly to touch the miracle unfolding within her; it is the song of Israel's rewarded longing for a saviour come to welcome in the promised age; it is the universal song of the oppressed and disempowered that proclaims God's favor on their behalf; it is a song of cosmic proportions that reverberates with the truth that divine life permeates and animates the hidden depths of matter.

It is a song of a woman. It is to her that I instinctively turn on this third Sunday of the season. She whose story, as an historic person, is so interwoven with the story of the Saviour who comes. She who is also a woman, one who knows, from within, the wondrous and awful experience of the kind of waiting that is like no other waiting: the waiting of pregnancy. She who has been painted, sculpted, etched, enameled, prayed, danced, and sung as one who is central to the season of Coming.

Protestant Christians have turned their attention to Mary primarily as the mother of the Lord, a simple Jewish girl who bore the child Jesus. Eastern Orthodox and Roman Catholic Christians have given more place to the symbolic significance of Mary. During the fourth century when the church in the East was hammering out its understanding of Christ, Mary was deemed *Theotokos*, Mother of God, God-bearer. She has also long been identified among Eastern Orthodox Christians as Sophia, God's wisdom. In the Western church she has taken on numerous aspects: throne of wisdom, queen of heaven, intercessor, mediatrix, co-redemptress, the woman of Revelation clothed by the sun, mother of the faithful and of the church, bride of Christ. The differing theological vantage points of the various branches of Christianity refract the image of this woman in varied ways. Be this as it may, in this season of vigil her presence is never far from any of us, either in scripture or in the music of the church's celebration.[22]

The rejoicing of Mary is the rejoicing of us all. The patristic and medieval church thought of her as humankind itself. She was the symbol of fallen humanity as it willingly entered into a restored relationship with God. She was the second Eve, who was to her predecessor what Christ, the second Adam, was to the first man. According to the fathers of the church, her "yes" to the divine initiative reversed the "no" uttered by Eve in the Garden. Her assent set in motion the events that made the incarnation, and thus the crucifixion and resurrection, possible. She was the sign of the readiness of humanity to bear the seed of the promise within its flesh. She was the one who changed the sadness of a fallen people into the rejoicing of a people redeemed. She was also creation itself. She was the fertile soil into which the divine seed was entrusted in order that it might grow and be harvested. She was the womb of the world in which the fetal Christ-life was taking shape. She was the one sung of in a 1634 Parisian Advent hymn: *Let the earth be opened and bud forth a Saviour!*

Perhaps for many Christians in the twentieth century such frankly symbolic interpretations of the images and persons depicted in the biblical text seem very foreign. In fact, they are foreign, for patristic and medieval canons of biblical interpretation were much different than our own. For generations of earlier Christians the texts of scripture were understood to have several distinct layers of meaning—literal, allegorical, moral, and mystical. The text could be read and commented on from any or all of these perspectives. This approach to scripture was not new to the patristic or medieval church. For the gospel accounts themselves functioned as interpretations of the Hebrew Bible by the Christian community reading back into them the divine story they believed was unfolding in the life and death of Jesus. Thus, for the writer of Luke, as Mary uttered the Magnificat she was not simply a young Jewish woman, she was the symbol of Israel receiving the promise. For medieval Christians this woman was a multivalent symbol allowing the faith community a glimpse into the mysterious depths of the incarnation so that they might catch sight there of what is hidden in the heart of God.

For centuries Christians have made it a practice to contemplate, to gaze deeply into, all the symbols of faith. In so doing they affirm that those images give us access into more than literal layers of meaning. And in metaphor and poetic refrain, generations of Christians have proclaimed the woman Mary as symbol of redeemed humanity and sign of creation renewed. Selected Marian praises from the Greek Agathistos hymn from the sixth century show this well.

> *Hail, thou, the restoration of the fallen Adam;*
> *hail, thou, the redemption of the tears of Eve.*
> *Hail, heavenly ladder by which God came down;*

hail, bridge leading from earth to heaven.
Hail, thou who revives the green fields of joy;
hail, thou who prepares a haven for souls.
Hail, land of promise; hail, thou from whom
flows forth milk and honey.
Hail, space for the uncontained God; hail,
door of solemn mystery.[23]

The compelling image of this pregnant woman has caused me as well to reflect upon the deeper meaning of the Advent season. In the Church of St. John on the campus where I teach is a side altar devoted to Mary. The statue resting in the niche there is one of the most graceful I have seen. One December afternoon, after a discouraging day of teaching, I found myself seated in front of it, staring blankly into space. Without an agenda for prayer beyond wanting to rest in a place of silence after too noisy a day, I found myself looking carefully for the first time at the statue before me. What I saw was a very young woman wearing a cloak draped over her shoulders. The folds of the cloak were drawn back to reveal the drape of an underdress which fell in soft folds to her feet. Beneath the underdress the weight of the statue's body seemed to lean back, producing the curved stance, so familiar in gothic iconography, that makes a figure look as if it is standing with all its weight upon one foot. This made the statue's belly curve slightly forward. Now it is not usual to find images of the pregnant Mary in our European influenced iconographical tradition. (Depictions of her visitation to Elizabeth are exceptions to this.) Free-standing images of the pregnant Mary are rare. I am not sure the sculptor of this piece intended this Mary to be obviously pregnant. But the folds of the cloak formed a frame around the curved belly, and I found myself contemplating not simply the body of a pregnant woman, but an image of the world very much like the photograph of our planet taken by the American astronauts several decades ago.

I began to see that within her body was the globe of the world. Within *our* body, within the womb of the world, the embryonic Christ lay curled. His fetal shape was discernible in the swirling eddies of oceans, continents, and clouds. We were carrying the Christ-life in us. The craggy mountains and fertile croplands of creation were his body, the world's waters his blood. Finite creation was ripe to bursting with the unimaginable presence of the infinite. The exquisite sonnet, The Annunciation, penned by the English poet John Donne sprang to mind.

> Salvation to all that will is nigh
> That All, which always is All ever where,
> Which cannot sin, and yet all sins must bear,
> Which cannot die, yet cannot choose but die,
> Lo, faithful virgin, yields himself to lie
> In prison, in thy womb; and though he there
> Can take no sin, nor thou give, yet he will wear
> Taken from thence, flesh, which deaths force may try.
>
> Ere, by the spheres time was created, thou
> Wast in his mind—which is thy son and brother,
> Whom thou conceivist-conceived; and the
> Father's Mother;
> Thou hast light in dark, and shut in little room
> Immensity, cloistered in thy dear womb.[24]

Donne's poetry captures the almost inexpressible paradox of divine becoming human. Immensity cloistered in a womb. Such are we. Such is the mystery we celebrate this season, immeasurable divine life measured to fit us. It is not simply Mary. She is all of us. We are her. This precious planet, this earth is the place of gestation. Matter is suffused and transfigured by the divine.

How little we really experience this—we who tend to treat matter as an inert substance there to be used or manipulated at will. Even our bodies we tend to treat at best as elaborate machines which we tinker with to achieve desired results. But the idea that matter is charged with spirit and alive with divine life is, for most of us, beyond our wildest schemes. But it has been intuited before and is imaged for us in this season of Advent in the rounded belly of a pregnant girl. Pierre Teilhard de Chardin, the French scientist and mystic, sensed this miracle and communicated it as he sang rhapsodically of the divine reality of matter in his *Hymn of the Universe.*

> I bless you, matter, and you I acclaim: not as the pontiffs of science or the moralizing preachers depict you, debased, disfigured–a mass of brute forces and base appetites–but as you reveal yourself to me today, in your totality and your true nature.
>
> You I acclaim as the inexhaustible potentiality for existence and transformation wherein the predestined substance germinates and grows.
>
> I acclaim you as the universal power which brings together and unites, through which the multitudinous monads are bound together and in which they all converge on the way of the Spirit.
>
> I acclaim you as the melodious fountain of water whence spring the souls of men and as the limped crystal whereof is fashioned new Jerusalem.
>
> I acclaim you as the divine milieu, charged with creative power, as the ocean stirred by the Spirit, as the clay moulded and infused with life by the incarnate Word.[25]

God is born in the body of the woman Mary, in the flesh of humankind, in the holy matter of the Universe. We proclaim the greatness of the Lord! Our spirits rejoice! Great things have been done for us! Holy is God's name!

Lifting Up the Lowly

Within the Roman rite, December 12 is celebrated as the Feast of Our Lady of Guadalupe. The memorial, of course, always falls within the Advent cycle. Many Christians of the United States will be familiar with this image of Mary, for it adorns innumerable churches, festival banners, and cultural mementos in any region whose art and culture are influenced by Mexico, or Central and South America. She is easily recognizable as a free-standing female figure wearing a blue star-flecked mantle over her head and shoulders and a pale red dress beneath. Surrounding her is a dazzling aura of gold, bright as the rays of sun. She stands atop a crescent moon borne up by the wings of a seraph-like creature. Her gaze is cast down and slightly to one side, and her hands are clasped in a gesture of prayer in front of her body just above a black band tied around her torso. The Lady of Guadalupe is perhaps the most powerful symbol of Advent rejoicing in all Christendom.

Her legend is this: Late in the year of 1531 an Indian peasant by the name of Juan Diego, a convert to the new faith brought to Mexico by the European conquerors, was going from his home in the poor section of Tepeyac, when he heard the strains of beautiful music. As he approached the source of the music, a beautiful woman appeared to him speaking his native tongue, Nahuatl. She told him to go to the archbishop of Mexico and tell him that the Virgin Mary, "Mother of the true God through whom one lives," wanted a temple built at the remote site where she was standing so that "she can show and give forth all my love, compassion, help, and defense to all the inhabitants of this land . . . to hear their lamentations and remedy their miseries, pain, and sufferings." Juan Diego, impressed with the lady's words, did as she asked. He found it difficult to get an audience with the archbishop, but when he finally did, his story was politely dismissed.

Twice more the lady appeared to the poor peasant, and twice more he tried to take her message to the ecclesiastical official. Discouraged, he pleaded with her that he was not the right person to fulfill her request since he was but a simple peasant, but she told him that he was indeed the one whom she had chosen. He went again to the episcopal palace. The harassed archbishop finally dismissed the persistent Juan Diego by telling him he would have to bring a sign from this Lady of his. The Lady then sent the peasant into a place where only desert plants existed, exhorting him to pick roses there. Such was not a place to look for roses, and certainly not at that time of year. Perplexed, he went and indeed found fresh red roses of Castille with dew still on their petals. Folding them in the *tilma* he wore round him like a cloak, he hurried to the archbishop's palace. When he unfolded the *tilma* not only did a cascade of roses fall to the floor, but the image of the lady as she had appeared to him was indelibly imprinted on the fabric itself.

Native response to this miracle was overwhelming; festivals, pilgrimages, and conversions to the religion of the Virgin took place in great numbers. Gradually the popular movement was incorporated into the official church, the Virgin eventually becoming the patron of the Americas. But her importance as a symbol of Advent rejoicing lies encoded in the iconography of the apparition and in her importance in the lives of the poor.

The significance of her appearance was evident to Juan Diego and his fellow countrymen, the conquered people of Europe's "New World." In the old Aztec religion music was the medium of divine communication; the lady appeared on the hill that was one of four sacred Aztec sacrificial sites, the sanctuary of the Mother of the Gods. Her dress and mantle were of colors sacred to the native peoples and connected with deity. The stars were associated with Aztec prophecies foretelling the collapse of their civilization and portending the beginning of a new era. She wore the black band of maternity showing that she was with child, a child whom she would give to the New World. She hid the sun (the principle Aztec deity) but did not extinguish it; she stood upon the moon (also a deity) but did not crush it, showing her to be greater than the native pantheon but not destructive of it. By wearing no mask she showed she was not a goddess, but that she was the compassionate mother. The fact that she requested a temple in her honor at the native site signified a new civilization in continuity within the past, yet radically transcending it.

The legend of Our Lady of Guadalupe is a cultural symbol of a conquered and oppressed people refusing to be destroyed by the dominant group. It is a sign of divine favor residing with the marginalized. It is a cry for dignity, for identity, and for liberation. She has become the symbol of the contemporary Latin American struggle to end the degradation and exploitation of the poor. Not only do the poor love her and respond to her message, but recent Latin American liberation theologians have understood her centrality in their vision of a society transformed to usher in God's saving reign of justice and peace.[26]

This Nahuatl Mary, some fifteen hundred years distant from Mary of Nazareth, sings the same Magnificat: He has thrown down the rulers from their thrones but lifted up the lowly. The hungry he has filled with good things. The rich he has sent away empty. All this is according to his promise.

The promise of a new creation, of the coming reign of God, is experienced when the hungry are fed, when those displaced by corporate interests are given back the access to land to feed their families, when power and wealth are equitably distributed, when those tortured and imprisoned for their beliefs or opposition to oppression are set free, when those living in fear of violence and the terrors of war are given peace. Out of the anguished and prolonged struggles of the poor and dispossessed of Latin America comes the cry: Rejoice! God's promise is of liberation, of a world renewed.

Four peasant women in the tiny war-torn village of Solentiname in Nicaragua in 1977 read the Bible together and reflected on Mary as she proclaimed the Magnificat.

Esperanza: "She praises God because the Messiah is going to be born, and that's a great event for the people. She calls God 'Savior' because she knows that the Son that he has given her is going to bring liberation."

Andrea: "She recognizes liberation. . . . We have to do the same thing. Liberation is from sin, that is, from selfishness, from injustice, from misery, from ignorance–from everything that's oppressive. That liberation is in our wombs, too, it seems to me."

Olivia: "She says that people will call her happy. . . . She feels happy because she is the mother of Jesus the Liberator, and because she also is a liberator like her son, because she understood her son and did not oppose his mission."

Gloria: "She spoke for the future, it seems to me, because we are just barely beginning to see the liberation she announces."[27]

As we keep watch during the vigil, we are called with these women to sing the song of rejoicing within our lives. The Magnificat is our canticle. It begins as a spiritual prayer and becomes the cry of the poor and ends as a hymn of praise. We rejoice for the fulfillment of the promise to Israel, for God's mercy and favor on behalf of the poor and oppressed, for the presence of divine life–hidden, active, and transforming the depths of matter itself. Rejoice!

Wonder

ADVENT'S FOURTH SUNDAY ALWAYS COMES UPON US as a surprise. Suddenly we are rushing headlong toward Christmas itself. Given the fact that the Feast of the Nativity is fixed on the liturgical calendar on December 25 and the beginning of the Advent season is a movable observance, on the fourth Sunday Christmas is often quite literally upon us within less than a week or even the very next morning. Suddenly the long wait is nearly over, and the wonder and sweetness of the day itself begins to be within our reach.

The activity around the Christmas tree in our house becomes intense. (It is our custom to put up the tree midway in the season.) Brightly wrapped packages, hidden until now in dark closets, mysteriously appear. Gifts from out-of-town relatives arrive via parcel post and are added to the jumble of reds, greens, and gold. Our youngest children greedily poke through the piles of treasures and memorize the feel of each gift marked with their names. Our oldest confines herself to discreetly shaking her presents when no one is looking. The sticky sweetness of brandied fruitcake and eggnog clings to our fingers and fills our mouths. The inexpressible memory-laden scent of fir tree permeates the air. We hang up mistletoe and spend the better part of a day surprising each other with kisses underneath its ribboned bough (which can get pretty chaotic when little brother gets into tormenting his older sisters).

By now promise and preparation and rejoicing give way to wonder. This is a season when the human heart allows itself to wonder, to marvel, to be surprised by awe and joy. I remember the wonder, as a little girl of five living in New York, of being taken to see Santa Claus at Macy's Department Store. I remember standing beside the loops of a velvet rope looking down a long line of parental legs and backs and seeing the faces of dozens of other youngsters peep around, disappear, and emerge again among gray and navy wool. I wore a white fur cap tied under my chin and proudly held a matching muff into which I could stuff my hands to lace together chilly fingers. My mother remembers that Macy's visit as an experience of exhausting waiting in an overheated store. Strangely, I have no memory of the actual moment during which I must have perched upon the plush knee of some out-of-work New York actor and whispered my secret wishes into a synthetic white beard. But I do remember the wonder of being there, the sense of something momentous about to happen, of some joy about to be revealed.

During Advent, we allow ourselves the liberty to become as little children, to see once again with simple eyes. Most of us gradually lose the capacity for wonder during our lives. We become cynical or bitter or, at least, realistic. Practicality and common sense dim our view. We forget how to dream. But during this season we are awakened once again.

Thomas Hardy, the English poet, managed to capture the poignant sense of this seasonal renewal of vision in "The Oxen."

> Christmas Eve, and twelve of the clock
>   Now they are all on their knees,
> An elder said as we sat in a flock
>   By the embers of hearthside ease.
>
> We picture the meek mild creatures where
>   They dwelt in their strawy pen,
> Nor did it occur to one of us there
>   To doubt they were kneeling then.
>
> So fair a fancy few would weave
>   In these years! Yet, I feel,
> If someone said on Christmas Eve,
>   Come; see the oxen kneel.

In the lonely barton by yonder coomb
      Our childhood used to know,
I should go with him in the gloom,
      Hoping it might be so.[28]

A Season of Dreams

When we read or hear the scriptures during Advent and Christmas, we are invited to experience them through wondering eyes and ears. We would certainly like to think we do so. After our canon of favorite carols sung this time of year (which includes, among others, "Silent Night, Holy Night," "O Come, All Ye Faithful," "Hark! the Herald Angels Sing," "It Came Upon the Midnight Clear," "Joy to the World, The Lord is Come," and "O Little Town of Bethlehem"), we have a secondary canon of seasonal music we like to dust off and play once again. Among these pieces is the Appalachian folk tune "I Wonder as I Wander," a plaintive melody that reminds us of the origins and ultimate outcome of the birth we so tenderly observe. As it is meant to do, this haunting tune always calls forth in me a sense of solitary and amazed wonderment.

I wonder as I wander out under the sky
How Jesus our Savior did come for to die
For poor, ornry people like you and like I
I wonder as I wander out under the sky.

When Mary birthed Jesus 'twas in a cow's stall
With wise men and farmers and shepherds and all
But high from the heavens a star's light did fall
And the promise of ages it then did recall.

Scripture too in this season is full of wonder, especially as evoked by tales of dreams and visions. The first chapter of Matthew tells us of Joseph's dream after he learned that Mary his wife to be was expecting a child.

> An angel of the Lord appeared to him in a dream and said,
> 'Joseph son of David, do not be afraid to take Mary home as
> your wife, because she has conceived what is in her by the Holy
> Spirit. She will give birth to a son and you must name him Jesus,
> because he is the one who is to save his people from their sins.' [29]

The second chapter tells that, similarly, after the birth of the
baby, Joseph is warned in another dream of the intent of King Herod
to destroy the child he fears will usurp him as king.

> The angel of the Lord appeared to Joseph in a dream and said,
> 'Get up, take the child and his mother with you, and escape into
> Egypt, and stay there until I tell you, because Herod intends to
> search for the child and do away with him.' [30]

The return of the family to the land of Israel is also initiated by
another dream, Joseph's angelic visitor telling him of the death of
Herod and the safety of returning to his native land (Matthew 2:9-
23). The infancy narratives are full of dreams. And it is not only in
scripture that we find evidence of dreams playing an important part in
the journey toward God. The history of our spiritual tradition is filled
with testimony that witnesses to the divine guidance of dreams.

Dreams are the stuff of the days before Christmas. But the
question is, do we really allow ourselves to dream, do we seriously
entertain the possibility that dreams still speak to us the words of
God? Or is prophetic and visionary dreaming something that ended
with the closing of the apostolic era? Are these stories we hear merely
quaint artifacts from a bygone age of innocence and superstition?
Have we grown up now and put aside such childish notions?

I would like to think that as we awaken to the wonder of this
moment, deep in the season of the Coming, we might awaken to the
wonder of our own capacity to dream. Both in the literal sense of our
sleeping dreams and in the figurative sense of our waking dreams. I am
not suggesting that we slavishly memorize a generic list of symbols

that appear in the unconscious and try to rigidly interpret the motives of our behavior by analyzing the contents of our night's sleep. Nor am I suggesting that we do a lot of positive visualization trying to realize our "dreams" of career success, financial stability, or fulfilling relationships. Rather, I am suggesting that most of us could be more alert to the gentle spiritual promptings and creative fantasizing that come from dreams, both night and day.

Today, certainly, serious discernment needs to be exercised in the interpretation of dreams, especially ones that seem to speak to more than the individual psyche and its spiritual unfolding. Christian tradition is full of accounts of people who claim to have dreamed authoritatively for the whole community or all humankind and who end up simply propagating their own interests or religious vision. I am not suggesting that everyone who remembers a dream should consider it to have been a divine visitation. Rather, I am suggesting that we might be more open, with careful guidance, to allowing the emergent contents of our dream consciousness to speak creatively to us, or to prompt us into a deeper knowledge of self and, ultimately, God.

First, we could better learn to attune ourselves to night dreams that seem to nudge us into a deeper relationship with God or which signal to us the ways we need to grow into love and faith and hope and grow out of the patterns of behavior and attitude that inhibit that growth. We could open ourselves in wonder to the images that well up as we sleep. For some of us, they may become friendly guides into the labyrinth of our own psyches. They may become for us companions as we wend our way through the deceits of our false selves toward the true self that knows itself to be a beloved child of God.

There are other sorts of dreams, more collective imaging, that we might well awaken to in this season as well. Most of us could be better waking dreamers of "holy dreams." Christians for centuries have been nurturing of such dreams, dreams of life lived bigger than life, dreams of being holy, of becoming saints. It has fallen out of favor perhaps because we, as a culture, have found new models to emulate that appeal more to our need for instant gratification and our desire for power and control. We dream of being film stars, and we long for the lives of the rich and famous with their glamorous homes and beautiful wardrobes and titillating romantic escapades. Or we idolize sports superstars or heroes of military victory. The Christian community has always offered cultural antiheroes whose lives and witnesses form the stuff of our holy dreams. No matter what the branch of Christendom and whether or not saints are officially designated as such within a denomination, saints have always been there as holy dreamers, fueling the imagination, giving flesh to our hidden dreams. Among the Quakers, it might be an Elizabeth Fry visiting the women inmates in the unspeakable conditions of Aldergate prison; among the Eastern Orthodox, a Macarius of Egypt in his desert hermitage practicing the prayer of the heart; among the Protestants during the Reformation, those English martyrs memorialized in *Fox's Book of Martyrs* who gave their lives for their confession under the reign of Mary Tudor–"bloody Mary"; among Roman Catholics, a Teresa of Avila, mystic and ardent reformer of her Carmelite monastic community. Whatever the texture or color, the power of a saint's life lies in its power to enflame our holy dreams.

In our media-dense culture we have grown somewhat dulled to the truth that images shape us. We are not only what we eat. We are formed by what we see, and we grow into what we see in our dreams. We tend to conceive of seeing as a neutral activity, and we debate endlessly the question whether viewing simulated violence on television or in movies actually contributes to an increase in violence among viewers. If consulted, the Christian tradition of prayer would offer a stinging critique of our somewhat naive ideas about the relationships between images, imagination, and human formation.

In that tradition, it has always been assumed that what one is shaped by what one sees.[31] Thus, in the early church, when Christians sought to live the new creation of the Christ-life, they fled to the deserts from the "world"—with its greed, pride, luxury, self-aggrandizement, and lust for power—to be remade in the image of Christ, into new creations formed by the Word, into persons of humility, compassion, and discernment. This flight from the "world" became institutionalized in the monastic life into which novices were initiated by being separated from the lives they had known and immersed in an entirely new set of circumstances and behaviors.

At the core of the new program of monastic formation was the action of the imagination. An entrant was presented with a program of scriptural reflection or (later in history) disciplined meditations (communal and individual) on the life of Christ which would serve to reshape her conception of who she was and for what purpose her life was intended. Not unlike the approach of contemporary cognitive psychology which attempts to reframe or reconstruct the psychic lens through which we filter reality in order to change our viewing, and thus our inner and outer lives, the ancient practices of Christian imaginative prayer redirect the energies of our persons to conform to the Christian vision of creation renewed.

To dream with and of the past and present saints of our churches is a spiritual discipline we would do well to practice. And many of us do, turning to mentors and models in our modern world whose lives give flesh to the promises of God. Not only can we admire Christians like Mother Teresa of Calcutta, Martin Luther King, Jr., Dietrich Bonhoeffer, Thomas Merton, Dorothy Day, and Dom Helder Camara, we can be changed by our familiarity with them. And we might well weave our holy dreams around the lives of our own local saints—a grandmother, a father, a pastor, a friend—who have been for us the image of God, who have enfleshed for us the vision of newness to which we are heir.

Advent is a time when our capacity to dream in new ways is awakened once more. We might do worse than to examine the contents of our waking dreams. What models do we strive to emulate? Which lives inform the choices we make in our own lives? Who are our mentors and our models? Or did we stop our holy dreaming in childhood? Is the sense of wonder and possibility something that died as we slipped into the realism and responsibility of adulthood? What might our mature holy dreams look like if we dared dream them now?

I have my own holy dream that I keep tucked away deep in the recesses of my heart. It is a dream that, as I have grown older, has more and more become woven into my conscious activities and attitudes. It is a dream that came to me in the form of a gesture, an action welling up from the underside of my conscious mind and expressing itself physically. It first came to me a number of years ago as I began an extended retreat. To get into the prayerful mood I thought was expected of me, I decided to go apart to a quiet place and be still. I first chose a nearby chapel. Then I tried the local park. Then an empty room. But wherever I went I found myself unable to sit, not because I was agitated or restless, but because what I seemed driven to do was stand, arms flung upward toward the sky. Like a lightning rod, I thought. Or a madwoman. What my body wanted to do was dip my fingertips way down to the earth, raise them slowly and majestically skyward, and stay stretched out as far as they would go. "Let us pray," were the words that accompanied the gesture. Not being one for charismatic forms of prayer, I was nonplused by the visceralness and persistence of this body prayer. I tried very hard to ignore it, divert myself from it, control it, and otherwise go about the business of being on retreat. The gesture would not let me. Bewildered, exhausted, fearful that I was half losing my sanity, I crawled in to see my retreat director at the end of the first week. His response was simple: "I suspect you are tired because you are resisting the movement of the Spirit in you."

Slowly, very slowly (it has taken years), I have begun to allow that gesture, that dream of being midway between earth and heaven and lifting up creation itself in prayer, to inspirit the many layers of my life. As teacher, spouse, parent, friend, spiritual companion, daughter, writer, retreat leader, and musician, that strange and powerful uplifting energy has motivated much of what I do. I have begun to be this dream.

The Dream of the Earth

What has become of wonder and dreaming in our modern lives? The root of contemporary religious aridity, I suspect, is the failure of our communal imaginations, our inability to dream holy enough dreams. As a human species, we are presently at a decisive juncture that is unprecedented in the course of history. We have the technological capability to destroy or irreparably alter the very composition of the earth itself. The building of military weaponry of unimaginable destructive potential by the world's dominant nations and the unbridled squandering of the earth's resources and pollution of the planet by the citizens of the earth place us at a new moment in time. These potentially catastrophic circumstances call forth from our religious communities new holy dreams and new imaginings. For it is our collective imagination, guided by various interests, some laudable, some not, that has brought us to this moment.

We must begin to envision ourselves differently than we have. We are all (hopefully) aware that the Christian tradition offers us an alternative perspective on the human person that counters the prevailing American individualistic ethos. Through that vision we begin to perceive that we are not simply by or for ourselves, but that we are part of one body, one dynamic organism that shares one life. St. Paul's letters give us the earliest testimony to this distinctive image of the body (1 Corinthians 12:12-30; Roman 12:3-8; Ephesians 2:11-22; Colossians 1:15-20). The church, both at the local level and as a worldwide communion, is an interdependent entity, sharing gifts and grace through the unity of the Spirit. Later tradition eased out the implications of Paul's body metaphor and came to understand the church as the "mystical body" in which salvation itself was virtually a communal undertaking, the spiritual energies and gifts of each member overflowing to contribute to the whole. The notion of the mystical body, when understood in its fullest implications, is a staggering one. It invites us into a vision of self that is essentially for and with others. We are not ruggedly scaling our lonely ways up the mountain tops of sanctification or, in the isolation of our hearts, surrendering to God's justification. What we ultimately are is the result of and contributes to the whole body. We are a part, and our life depends on the extent to which we see that clearly and live out of the vision of an interconnected spiritual web of grace and gift.

As the image of the mystical body is lived into in a prayerful way, it opens out into a more and more expansive vision. In our shrinking global community it becomes increasingly difficult to clearly delineate the lines between us and them, between the saved and the damned, between the believer and the non-believer. Contemporary theology is engaged in wrestling with the distinctive message of Christian revelation in this pluralistic world. Be that as it may, on the experiential level, we now find ourselves as different religious traditions, cultures, and nationalities suddenly thrown together with a new sense of our shared identity as inhabitants of an earth whose potential destruction profoundly affects us all. We are part of one body, one created organism, upon which we are equally dependent. We can no longer act as nations with ultimate interests at variance from other nations, nor can we act as cultural groups whose distinctiveness cuts us off from the shared business of living on this earth in a way responsible not only for future human generations, but the future generations of all life forms. We can no longer see ourselves as users of an earth that we perceive to be inert matter. Modern science instead invites us into a new appreciation of the universe itself as a magnificent living organism of which we are an extravagantly unique part. We humans are an experiment of the divinely-authored universe itself, an experiment in self-reflective awareness. Of all the life forms known to us, only human beings have the capacity to reflect on and thus bring consciousness to bear on existence. Only human beings have the capacity for praise, for wonder, and for holy dreams. Only human beings can imagine, and thus bring into being, the fruition or the failure of the promises hidden in the heart of God. We are the heart and mind of creation, saying yes or saying no to our ultimate destiny as God's beloved community. We are the space where creation dreams. Our dreaming is formative. It directs our formidable energies into the path of peace or the path of destruction.[32]

Our tradition has the germ of a holy image in the metaphor of the mystical body which might well be brought to fruition now. Extended beyond narrow confines that limit it simply to the church community, the mystical body is a metaphor that might speak to us quite literally of our embodied faith, and allow us to see ourselves as parts of a whole creation on which we are dependent and which is dependent upon us and our holy dreaming for its continued life.

Angelic Messengers

In scripture angels are often bearers of wondrous news. During the Advent season, bell choirs and Christmas carolers never seem to tire of performing the ebullient "Angels We Have Heard on High."

Angels we have heard on high
sweetly singing o'er the plains,
and the mountains in reply
echoing their joyous strains.

Its glorious refrain, *Glo-o-o-o-o-o-o-o-o-o-o-o-o-o-o-ri-a,* *in* *excelsis De-e-o!* trills down the scale, sending voices or bell tones tumbling down on top of one another. It is a joyous expression of the seasonal spirit. One that forces us to lift up our heads and our hearts to listen to the angels' song.

Perhaps we should look up more frequently, for angels are everywhere during the season–in scripture and in carols, as well as hanging in delicate festoons of glass and *papier-mache* upon our trees. The Christmastide angels in Matthew's Gospel, as we have seen, are the shadowy figures that show themselves only in dreams. In the infancy narratives of Luke, however, they appear out of the clear blue sky, as it were. They approach Zechariah, John the Baptist's father, before the birth of his son.

> At the hour of incense, the whole congregation was outside, praying.
> Then there appeared to [Zechariah] the angel of the Lord, standing on the right of the altar of incense. The sight disturbed Zechariah and he was overcome with fear.[33]

Angelic visitation is likewise central to the announcement of the Advent of Jesus himself and the news of the holy birth.

> In the sixth month the angel Gabriel was sent by God to a town of Galilee called Nazareth, to a virgin betrothed to a man named Joseph, of the House of David, and the virgin's name was Mary. He went in and said to her, 'Rejoice, so highly favored! The Lord is with you.' She was deeply disturbed by these words and asked herself what this greeting could mean. . . .[34]
> In the countryside close by there were shepherds who lived in the fields and took it in turns to watch their flocks during the

night. The angel of the Lord appeared to them and the glory of
the Lord shone around them. They were terrified. . . .[35]

The word of God comes through the medium of angel
messengers. It was with a sense of fear and a sense of wonder that
Zechariah and Mary and the shepherds received their strange and
luminous guests. Their shared fear was not the fear that comes when
unnatural or eerie things occur, but the awestruck fear that is
engendered by the holiness of the divine itself. And they listened. They
received the angels' messages, allowing the magnitude of what was
communicated to change the course of their lives.

The narrative of Luke paints for us a picture of persons who
were willing to look up in wonder and to truly hear. Can we be such
people as well? One of the most beloved and dramatic of Christmas
hymns, "O Holy Night," contains a phrase that distills for me the
attitude of wonder intrinsic to the season of waiting.

> *Fall on your knees,*
> *Oh hear the angel voices!*
> *O night divine,*
> *O night when Christ was born!*

Angelology as a theological discipline has fallen into oblivion in
most Christian denominations today. There was a time, in the
biblical, patristic, and medieval eras, when the sense of angels as
hovering, active presences in the world was very real to people. Today
we tend to live in a much "flatter" (one-dimensional) world when it
comes to our imaginations. We tend not to be sensitive to the invisible
reality that hides behind the visible. Literalists to the core, we live out
of only what can be validated empirically. But other ages have been
more alive to mystery, more open to wonder. In our fear of
superstition (which, in fact, can be a real concern) we perpetually live
in a modern mental universe stripped of the numinous presence of the

divine. One of the challenges of the Advent season is to awaken once more to the breathless apprehension of childhood, alive to secret messages, to the whispers of hidden voices and the touch of God.

Medieval scholastic theologians carefully defined the nature of angels, as they defined everything else. They saw them basically as non-corporeal intelligences whose nature was intermediate between divine and human. They divided them into various hierarchies, following the speculations of a sixth century Syrian monk, Dionysius the Pseudo-Areopagite, thus giving us the various rankings of celestial beings that we sing out from the pages of our hymn books: seraphim, cherubim, thrones, dominions, powers, authorities, principalities, archangels, and angels. When all this is said and done, in the tradition, angels are messengers of God. Winged words. Hovering visitations. They are the medium through which God touches our lives. But we must be alert for their arrival, open to hear their words.

In this season especially, we are invited to be alive to their nearness, anticipating their arrival in our time. Who then are our angels that come to us, as it were, out of the clear blue sky? Who in our lives are the messengers of God? Who are those around us–spouse, children, parents, friends, colleagues, members of the congregation, strangers–who come to us as the medium through which God wishes to touch our lives? Have we eyes capable of the simple vision and hearts capable of the wonder needed to discern what they have to say?

My husband recently shared an experience of being visited by angels. He recognized their presence only in retrospect. Things had been going badly for him at work for considerable time. (He is a social justice educator.) There were interpersonal difficulties with fellow workers, cutting criticisms of work he had done, and financial readjustments that caused a restructuring of his organization. His position was essentially eliminated, and he found himself, in mid-life, profoundly doubtful of his own abilities, confused about what was happening, angry and resentful at everyone and everything, and unclear about who he was. In the midst of it he discovered himself praying the cry of the psalmist, "Why have you abandoned me?" He listened, but there seemed to be no response. Then, perhaps a year later, he had an opportunity to look back prayerfully on this arduous time and discovered that indeed he had received an answer to his prayer.

Two acquaintances, both persons he respected highly, had unexpectedly contacted him during the difficulties and expressed their solidarity with him at a profound level. One, an older black woman, had extended herself: "You have a beautiful soul. I love you. You are my brother." The other, a younger man whose dedicated work with the poor was an inspiration to my spouse, affirmed, "You are so talented. You have so many gifts. I know it is a struggle. I just want you to know that I love you." Looking back, my husband saw that these two friends were indeed angels in disguise. They were the response to his lonely, abandoned prayer. He was not forgotten; he had been visited. The message of the angels was a message of love.

When have we been visited so that we might truly join our voices with the graceful melody of the nineteenth century carol?

> It came upon the midnight clear
> that glorious song of old,
> from angels bending near the earth,
> to touch their harps of gold:
> "Peace on the earth, goodwill to men,
> From heaven's all-glorious King."
> The world in solemn stillness lay,
> To hear the angels sing.

It is a season of wonder and a season of angelic visitation. Let us look up.

THE COMING

And you, high eternal Trinity,
acted as if you were drunk with love,
infatuated with your creature.
When you saw that this tree could bear no fruit
but the fruit of death
because it was cut off from you who are life,
you came to its rescue
with the same love with which you had created it:
you engrafted your divinity into the dead tree
   of our humanity.
O sweet tender engrafting!
You, sweetness itself, stooped to join yourself
   with our bitterness.
You, splendor, joined yourself with darkness;
you, wisdom, with foolishness;
you, life, with death;
you, the infinite, with us who are finite.
What drove you to this
to give back life to this creature of yours
that had so insulted you?
Only love, as I have said,
and so by this engrafting, death is destroyed.[36]

CATHERINE OF SIENA
(1347-1380)

Silence

AT LAST WE ARE HERE. We have arrived at the moment of the Coming. We hover at the threshold of the birth. We have lived these previous days of pregnant waiting, ripe with our hidden secret and heavy with longing. The days of waiting–with their varied textures of joy, wonder, anxiety, and bustling preparation–now seem distant, dwarfed by the magnitude of the reality present to us.

There is a strange timeliness to the experience of the actual coming of a child. Most women who have borne children can attest to this fact. In the days of waiting, time, as medium of change, dominates consciousness. The new life growing inside you profoundly shapes your own life. A new self-concept grows, a new sense of embodiment impinges on consciousness, a new "other" holds sway from within. You are not who you thought you were. Rather, you are a person whose identity–psychic, spiritual, and physical–is intimately linked to another person. You are persons overlapped in time and space, sharing breath and blood and heartbeat. During the waiting most women are keenly aware of time. Time measured out between obstetrical appointments, time weighed in added pounds and unwieldiness, time parceled out by the growing awareness of presence– from the first moth-like flutters of the "quickening" to the astonishing protrusions of stretching feet and arms. Submerged in an ocean of time–transformed by it, submissive to it–your deepest desire is cast like a tiny float out on its shoreless waves.

Suddenly the coming is upon you, and time dissolves. There is only the present in its gleaming, stark clarity. No past, no future, there is only now–this time which is strangely timeless in its intensity. There are as many different experiences of birth as there are women, but for all of them the waiting is over. The promised one bursts forth, new life sings out, the primal rush of blood and water carries the miracle into our arms. It is a moment whose mystery is timeless.

Three Births

It was the custom in medieval Christianity to celebrate three masses on the Feast of Christmas, one at midnight, one at dawn, and one at noon on Christmas Day. Each of the celebrations had its particular focus and medieval preachers like John Tauler, fourteenth century German cleric, exercised their exegetical skills in delineating them.

> Today Holy Christendom commemorates a threefold birth, which should so gladden and delight the heart that, enraptured with joyful love and jubilation, we should soar upward with sheer gratitude and bliss . . . .
>
> The first birth, and the most sublime, is that in which the Heavenly Father begets His only Son within the divine Essence, yet distinct in Person. The second birth we commemorate is that of maternal fruitfulness brought about in virginal chastity and true purity. The third birth is effected when God is born within a just soul every day and every hour truly and spiritually, by grace and out of love. These are the three births observed in today's three Holy Masses.[37]

Tauler, and others like him, employing the biblical scholarship of their times (which, it will be remembered, acknowledged mystical, allegorical, and moral as well as literal meanings of scriptural texts) saw the Feast of the Nativity as a lens into the multi-layered mystery of divine birth: in the Godhead, in the womb of Mary, in the soul of the individual Christian. Through this lens one could view the workings of the Trinity itself. The first birth explored the creative fecundity of the Father, the second heralded the Advent of the Son, the third dealt with the fertile indwelling of the Holy Spirit in the hearts and minds of humankind. All three persons of the Trinitarian God were envisioned as creatively active in bringing forth new life.

Medieval writers also saw these births (as well as the three persons of the Trinity) as corresponding to what they conceived to be the three parts of the human soul: memory, intellect, and will.

The time of each of the masses had symbolic significance for each of the three births. The first took place in the darkness of midnight, corresponding to the secrecy and hiddenness of the inaccessible and incomprehensible birth eternally taking place within the mystery of the Godhead. Dawn was the hour for the celebration of the second birth, when the Word become flesh appeared among us. Half in darkness, half in light, the dawn mass symbolized the mystery of the incarnation, which in its origins was shrouded in dark nighttime mystery; but in its fruit was known clearly in the day. The bright light of noon illuminated the feast of the third birth—the birth of God in the human soul—which continues to take place, in the view of medieval Christendom, through an attitude of prayerful contemplation and receptivity to the indwelling of the Spirit.

Silence

Our Advent and Christmastide liturgies are dominated by the testimony of the Gospels of Luke and Matthew. But at least once during the season we hear from the fourth evangelist, John. For a moment we face backwards, as it were, away from the anticipatory spirit that beckons us into the wonder of the first and the majesty of the Second Coming of Christ. In the Prologue to John's Gospel, we look back liturgically to the origins of all things, into the abyss of divinity before creation itself.

> In the beginning was the Word:
> the Word was with God
> and the Word was God.
> He was with God in the beginning.
> Through him all things came to be,
> not one thing had its being but through him.[38]

We pause for a while to reflect upon what the medieval world understood to be the dynamic potency of the trinitarian God. This first, eternal birth of the Word in "the bosom of the Father" was the point of entry into the mystery of the Coming. Tauler elaborated on it in this way.

> Note that the Father, distinct as the Father, turns inward to Himself with His divine intellect and penetrates in clear self-beholding the essential abyss of His eternal Being. In this act of pure self-comprehension He utters Himself completely by a Word, and the Word is His Son. And the act whereby He knows Himself is the generation of the Son in eternity. Thus He rests within Himself in the unity of essence and He flows out in the distinction of Persons.[39]

It is not enough to contemplate the astonishing fact of the incarnation on this day of birth. We are invited, through the window of the scriptures proclaimed in our Christmastide services, to extract ourselves for a moment from the medium of time and venture into timelessness. There is in this season an intimation of the bursting forth from time's duration into the eternity that is both our origin and end.

We enter into an experience of God that, for all the intellectual adventuring and the theological ponderings of the Christian centuries, is ultimately beyond our ability to conceptualize. Here, for a moment, in this season dense with signs, wonders, images, stories, and revelation, we are turned about and find ourselves gazing speechless into the recesses of the cosmos, before eternity uttered a Word. Johannes Tauler and his fourteenth century contemporaries were intrepid explorers in this eternal realm and they made bold assertions about the inner workings of divinity. Yet they ended always with the same intuition: it is in silence that we become most intimate to the source of all life. A fellow Germanic countryman of Tauler's known as

Angelus Silesius, who lived three centuries later, shared this sentiment in the form of an epigram.

> God far exceeds all words that we can here express.
> In silence He is heard, in silence worshipped best.[40]

Meister Eckhart, Tauler's older contemporary and mentor, pushed this apprehension to its fullest limit. He held that behind and beyond the self-expression of God in revelation lies a hidden, unexpressed, essential reality. The God about whom we know something is God, but beyond God is the Godhead, God in pure essence, defined as the origin of all things beyond God. We know God through our capacity to conceptualize, to image, and to reason. We come into relationship with the Godhead only by unknowing, by emptiness and in silence. Eckhart, Tauler, and Angelus Silesuis are, of course, part of a long tradition in Christian mysticism which would tease us into divine intimacy through the "via negativa," through the medium of silence and self-emptying.

Midnight on Christmas Eve is the still, silent point of the entire Advent and Christmas season. We turn back to gaze upon the cosmic origins of our celebration. We are vaulted beyond time into eternity.

Our contemporary world is hardly a silent one. Most Americans live in urban centers. On the rare occasions when we venture out into the countryside or into genuine wilderness we may suddenly be aware of a depth of silence to which we are rarely exposed. Most of us screen out the constant hum of traffic and industrial noise that assaults us at all times. And we have become accustomed to filling our homes and public places with the audio input of television and radio waves. From the raucous rhythms of a crowded trendy club over which it is nearly impossible to speak to the calming hum of the Muzak that floats down the aisles of our grocery stores, we are a culture that insists on filling silence with sound. We tend to think of silence as an awkward hole in a conversation that must be filled in or a mistaken moment in a church service when somebody forgot what was supposed to come next.

Yet, in the history of our Christian tradition of prayer, silence is the most precious of mediums through which we can be initiated into the life of God. The tradition of contemplative silence dates from at least the third and fourth centuries when ardent Christians seeking the true Christ-life fled to the deserts of Egypt, Syria, and Palestine to be remade in the image of God through what they termed ascetic martyrdom. In solitary caves or huts they fasted, slept little, plaited baskets, and prayed. Their prayer was most often the prayer of one who listens in silence. Silence was for them the safest way to go to God, and they cultivated it assiduously. The cryptic *Sayings of the Fathers* preserves their struggle in word-pictures.

> A certain brother went to Abbot Moses in Scete, and asked him for a good word. And the elder said to him: Go, sit in your cell, and your cell will teach you everything.[41]

> It was said of Abbot Agatho that for three years he carried a stone in his mouth until he learned to be silent.[42]

> A certain one told this story: There were three earnest men, that loved one another, and they became monks. And one of them chose to bring to accord such as take the law of each other, according to that which is written: *Blessed are the peace-makers.* The second chose to visit the sick. But the third went away to be quiet in solitude. Now the first, toiling amid the contentions of men, was not able to appease them all. And overcome with weariness, he came to him who tended the sick, and found him also failing in spirit, and unable to carry out his purpose. And the two agreed together and went away to see him who had withdrawn into the desert, and they told him their tribulations. And they asked him to tell them how he himself had fared. And he was silent for awhile, and then poured water into a vessel and said, "Look upon the water." And it was murky. And after a little

while he said again, "Look now, how clear the water has become." And as they looked in to the water they saw their own faces, as in a mirror. And then he said to them, "So is he who abides in the midst of men: because of the turbulence, he sees not his sins: but when he hath been quiet, above all in solitude, then does he recognise his own default."[43]

For the abbas (fathers) and ammas (mothers) of the desert, solitude with its silence was a creative medium, a forge of transformation through which the false self in its adaptation to the pride, luxury, lust for power, and greed of the "world" was melted away in the fires of spiritual discernment. One emerged from the silence as a transformed self, newly formed in the image of God in Christ: a person of humility, compassion, and responsiveness to the Word of God. Silence was, in this early ascetic tradition, much more than not speaking. It was mostly a quality of heart. It was the creation of an inner space where genuine listening could take place. The ammas and abbas knew that in silence the Word most readily takes root.

To begin to enter into the profound silence that resides in the depths of our beings is to begin to enter the realm of the Godhead beyond God. Beyond speech, beyond apprehension is a realm of generative actuality, the realm of essential being out of which the Word is eternally begotten. Our silence is both the empty pathway by which we venture most surely into the divine mystery and the clear road by which the Word proceeds most directly into our hearts.

The monastic traditions of Christianity have continued to live the silent wisdom of the desert, creating oases of silent listening in the midst of or on the margins of the frenetic motion and insistent noise of cultural environments both past and present. Despite their varied rules and customs, these monastic traditions continue to cultivate a silence that is timeless. They dip down into the still center of the human person where it opens out into the stillness of eternity. They celebrate the fecund emptiness, the ultimate simplicity out of which we all come and to which we ultimately return.

Perhaps, at this still point of the season in the dark midnight, when time is suspended and we find ourselves gazing speechless into the abyss, we might be well to reflect on silence. I sometimes assign my university theology students a journal question that forces them to think about their experience of silence as a medium of self and religious awareness. With a few exceptions (in cases where a student is either afraid of being silent, or so unaccustomed to it that they cannot conceive of it in a positive way), most young people appreciatively recount their rare encounters with silence. A late night drive home after work where one can "sort out the day," an early morning run through streets before the city is awake, camping in the awesome stillness of the Rocky Mountains, sitting alone quietly by a pond, entering an empty church—these are recalled as precious experiences of renewal or insight or spiritual quickening. Yet how infrequently we integrate these experiences into the fabric of our daily lives. How little we seek to live out of the silence. How unfamiliar we are, as a culture, with the spaciousness and creativity of silence.

Our Christian monastic traditions have tended to cultivate environments of silence in which individual persons can share together a structured common lifestyle which frees each one to turn ears and lay hands upon the heartbeat of God. Yet this type of silent listening is not essentially communal. There is, however, one small pocket of Christian life in which shared silence is deliberately nurtured. Among the Society of Friends (the Quakers) worship most often consists of waiting together in silence. The classic Quaker silent meeting is an experience of the whole community coming into the presence of the inward Christ, where all come to know each other in that which is eternal. The theological assumption underlying this ritual-less ritual is that the truly Christian life is one lived in reliance on the "Inner

Light" of the living Christ who speaks most authentically in the silence of the soul. The silence is understood at that level not to be private but most deeply shared; for at the heart of the person dwells Christ, who speaks not simply for the comfort of each, but for the good for all. Listening that takes place in a silent meeting is thus not primarily a listening to the Word as it may be received idiosyncratically. It is a listening to the Word who binds all hearts and minds Godward and directs the common life of the community in the ways of love and peace, drawing persons from their separateness into solidarity.[44]

At the still point of the Advent and Christmas season dwells that silence which is at once the incommunicable voice of the Godhead, the transforming fire of our true self, and the common ground upon which we all most authentically meet.

As a child I had my first simple glimpses into the awesome generativity of the silence hidden in the dark of midnight at Christmas. My earliest (before the age of four) seasonal memories are of late Christmas Eve night. My parents and I lived in a small one-bedroom wooden house in central Los Angeles. I slept in one alcove of a long front parlor, and from my bed I could look the length of the room past the front door into the area that served as a living room. During Advent we would set up our Christmas tree smack in the middle of the round living room rug. On Christmas Eve, I would be put to bed with firm instructions to go to sleep and told that when I wakened in the morning, the tree branches would be sprouting presents. Of course, I tried to stay awake to witness the mysterious arrival of the gifts.

The room was pitch black except for the warm illumination of the tree lights glowing from the far end of the room. At first, I would sit myself upright to await the event, but soon the weight of my sleepiness pulled me lower and lower onto the bed until I was finally lying flat, my head strained sideways so I could still see the glow of the lights through half-closed eyes. What was really so riveting about waiting quietly in that darkened room was not the thought of the gifts (although that had obvious appeal), but the experience of watching and waiting in that unfamiliar nighttime silence. I would stay awake long enough to hear my parents turning in for the night, then to hear the late night sounds of the city gradually diminish, until finally I was wrapped in a thick, snug blanket of silence, the likes of which I had never known. My breathing alone punctuated the quiet. Then even that seemed to fade away.

That silence encased a numinous mystery far greater than any tasty candy or bright toy that might appear the next morning. It was alive with its own incommunicable splendor–pregnant with something I had no words for, no images to express. I never managed to stay awake long enough to view whatever really happened there in the quietest hour of night, but I was close to it, I knew, in the silence itself–breathing in, breathing out, keeping watch, keeping vigil for the Coming.

Poverty

WHEN MY ELDEST DAUGHTER WAS A TODDLER she had a special fondness for the carol, "Away in the Manger," and we would sing it together to the rhythm of our rocking chair each night in Advent as she lay curled in my arms in the warmth of her darkened room.

> *Away in a manger, no crib for a bed,*
> *the little Lord Jesus lay down his sweet head.*
> *The stars in the sky looked down where he lay,*
> *the little Lord Jesus, asleep on the hay.*
>
> *The cattle are lowing, the poor baby awakes,*
> *but little Lord Jesus, no crying he makes;*
> *I love thee, Lord Jesus, look down from the sky*
> *and stay by my cradle till morning is nigh.*

These tender lyrics, which legend claim were penned by the great Protestant reformer Martin Luther for his own small children at Christmastide, give voice to some of our most cherished impressions of the season. For all the glorious and awesome dimensions of the Advent and Christmas cycle, for many Christians it is the gentle vision of the tiny child wrapped in swaddling clothes lying in the manger that is the most apt expression of the spirit of the season. For Christmas is the celebration of God's becoming poor for us, God's entering into the limitations of our humanness, God's becoming a child. In our homes and in our churches we reconstruct the scene that centuries of prayerful Christian imagination has constructed from the second chapter of Luke's Gospel.

> Now at this time Caesar Augustus issued a decree for a census of the whole world to be taken. This census–the first–took place while Quirinius was governor of Syria, and everyone went to his own town to be registered. So Joseph set out from the town of Nazareth in Galilee and travelled up to Judaea, to the town of

David called Bethlehem, since he was of David's house and line, in order to be registered with Mary, his betrothed, who was with child. While they were there the time came for her to have her child, and she gave birth to a son, her first-born. She wrapped him in swaddling clothes, and laid him in a manger because there was no room for them at the inn.[45]

With ritual prayerfulness each year, individuals, families, and congregations unwrap the ceramic or wooden or plaster of paris figurines from their nativity sets and re-create together the long-ago scene. My favorite crèche scenes in churches are always those that nestle the Christ child and Mary and Joseph beneath a forest of fresh cut evergreen trees or boughs, adding the pungent aroma of fir or pine to the church smells of chill stone or wood or carpet that envelop the scene. With softened hearts each year, year after year, we lead our smallest children by hand up the aisle before or after worship services to gaze with gentle eyes and speak with hushed voices of the fragile baby and the man and woman wrapped in adoration there. It is a ritual of astonishing power that never fails to draw us into the mystery of the season. At the Old Mission Church in Santa Barbara, where my husband and children and I were parishioners for a decade, it was the custom to set up a life-size nativity set on the sloping expanse of the lawn that skirted the front of the church. A kneeling Mary and Joseph and three ornately attired foreign-looking royalty were set up beneath a three-sided stable. All were facing expectantly toward a hay-stuffed crib that remained empty until the evening of December twenty-fourth. Penned in small yards on either side of the stable were live donkeys and sheep. There was never an hour during the last week or so of Advent until Epiphany when you could not see children and their parents or adults alone hanging over the railing and entering with something like wonder (even those who had come primarily to pet the animals) into the scene depicted there.

There is an astonishing beauty to a little child. For this one liturgical moment we all pause in awe. And, for all that we know about that one particular long-ago child to be, and as much as we feel called upon to reflect on the implications of that one long-ago birth, there is an instant in this season when *all* births, *all* small children, the miracle of each new life, despite its poor fragility, is felt and reaffirmed. When a mother or father or a grandparent takes his or her small charge by chubby fingers up to the altar rail to meet the baby Jesus, there is a rush of memory of infant hands and limbs once held in loving arms. As we sing our most cherished Christmas lullabies, we mingle our memories of newborns swaddled in our arms with our memories of the Mother Mary as she cradles her own first born child.

> *Silent night, holy night,*
> *all is calm, all is bright*
> *round yon virgin mother and child.*
> *Holy infant, so tender and mild,*
> *Sleep in heavenly peace,*
> *Sleep in heavenly peace.*

Some of the most poignant of Christmas songs with which worshippers over the centuries have given voice to their God-ward love are the nativity ballads and lullabies. A sixteenth century dance tune provides the musical setting for England's favorite cradle song.

> *What child is this who laid to rest,*
> *on Mary's lap is sleeping?*
> *Whom angels greet with anthems sweet,*
> *while shepherds watch are keeping?*
>
> *This, this is Christ the King,*
> *Whom shepherds guard and angels sing;*
> *Haste, haste to bring him laud,*
> *The babe, the son of Mary.*

A fourteenth century German cradle-rocking song records a homey conversation between the mother Mary and her husband.

"Joseph, dearest, Joseph mine.
Help me cradle the child divine;
God reward thee and all that's thine
In paradise," so prays the mother Mary.

"Gladly, dear one, lady mine,
Help I cradle this child of thine;
God's own light on us both shall shine
In paradise," so prays the mother Mary.

From fifteenth century Cologne comes the haunting carol:

Lo, how a rose e're blooming
from tender stem hath sprung!
Of Jesse's lineage coming,
as those of old have sung.
It came a floweret bright,
Amid the cold of winter,
When half spent was the night.

At the heart of the season is our shared recognition of the incommunicable experience of the birth of a child. In this experience we intuitively grasp both the awesome wonder and responsibility of becoming bearers of new life as well as the great fecundity of the creation itself which continues to unfold in fullness from the poorest and most fragile of beginnings. The early Western church fixed the Feast of the Nativity at the time of the winter equinox, presumably to assimilate non-Christian religious observances held that time of the year into the new faith. In the shortened days of winter light (at least in the Northern hemisphere), the Christian community established the feast which celebrates the dawning of light in the darkness. At a very deep level, this feast is a reenactment of the ancient cosmic mystery of life arising out of death, of the renewal of creation itself through the process of generativity. We, as part of this most amazing creation, our earth, participate in the ongoing renewal of life itself that takes place within the structure of stars, the microbes, plant life and our own bodies. There is nothing "merely biological" about this miracle of new life unless we would refuse to look with eyes of wonder upon the pulsing dynamic of the universe present in our own bodies, whose mysteries invite us to contemplate the mystery of divine life itself.

God Made Flesh

A number of years ago I attended a retreat at a Benedictine monastery on the coast of rural Massachusetts. It was a women's retreat sponsored by the graduate school that my husband was attending and where I was teaching part-time. Most of our time as a group was spent together at the retreatants' cottage where we prayed and engaged in faith sharing, but we were free before or after sessions to cross the street and attend any of the daily offices being held in the monastery up the hill. Since I do appreciate the singing of the liturgical hours, I frequently made my way up to the church in the chill hours of dawn and dusk. It had been a brisk New England winter so far: snow was hard packed on the ground and gusts of icy wind made the warmth of the little church or the retreat house welcome refuges after my walks to or fro. One evening as I was leaving the monastery from the vespers service with a small cluster of worshippers, an older monk burst in from out-of-doors and hailed us. Did we want to go down to the barn with him and see the new lamb that had been born? A couple of people begged off, saying they had a bit of a drive to make in the gathering, sleety dark. But one or two others and I took the good brother up on his invitation.

He led us out behind the church and through the snowy woods to a low wooden lean-to that served as a barn for the community's livestock. Being far from the nighttime glow of the urban landscape, it was incredibly dark and we found ourselves nervously staying close to our host lest we lose our way in the gloomy shadows of the trees. The entrance to the barn was low and we had to bend over to squeeze through the door. Once inside, we found ourselves in another world. In contrast with the frozen, dark forests which opened out into the immensity of a star-studded sky we were suddenly in a low, tight place of warmth and light. One bare light bulb hung boldly from the rafters, sending uneven rays of illumination over a hay-strewn welter of fences and cribs and a variety of small farm animals. The striking warmth of the barn came not from any artificial source, but from the bodies and the breaths of the animals themselves. A visceral sense of the creatureliness of that place came over me. The odors of food and feces, the sounds of shuffling, lowing and bleating, the feel of thick fleece as a sheep eased her way behind me in the crowded space, the sight of dozens of bright peering creature eyes and pointed ears all turned in my direction–all of it made me vividly aware of myself and the animals as being alive, enfleshed. And there she was. One panting, tired ewe wedged between a fence post and a pile of hay, her still-wet newborn lamb bleating and groping for a teat on her outstretched belly.

I do not think I had ever really imagined the infancy scriptures before, at least not as stories that were truly enfleshed. If I had gazed on them, it was as theological insights or as rather sentimental plaster-of-paris tableaux. But suddenly I was there, imagining that birth of nearly two millennia ago. I who had access to the privacy and hygienic conditions of a birthing room in a modern hospital, I who had friends nearby and a staff of trained personnel, I was imagining a young woman far from home and family, amid the strong stench of animal debris and the warm clouds of animal breath hanging in the frozen night air, in frightened labor with her first child. It was a vision that took my breath away.

Of course, I could have returned to the retreat house from my reverie and reminded myself that the infancy passages in scripture need not be understood as literal fact, and that centuries of religious imagination have added details to our mental pictures–winter snow and pine forests for instance–that could not be historically accurate. But quantifiable data is not the main point of such scripture passages. They are poetic narrative windows onto truths only the language of poetry and music can convey. My and others' recreative entry into this religious moment on the property of the Benedictine monks or kneeling at the altar rail of a community church are moments of profound, creative insight. We enter into the ultimate meaning of an event through the language of story, both stories of long ago and our own stories. We enter into a prism of images through which the deeper meaning of our personal lives, our shared lives, and our greater life in God is refracted.

What I saw that night in that close, animal-packed barn was that God was made flesh. God become human. God entered into our "poverty," all that is most creaturely, most bodily, most intimately us. I smelled it and felt it and heard it. And I saw it with the eyes of my heart. As close as I was to that panting ewe, so close was God to my humanity. It is all too easy for us, and we do it with alarming frequency, to want to divorce our sense of God from our everyday, material lives. God we associate with private, "spiritual" longings, with good and perfect otherworldly thoughts. But this is not the stunning insight of our faith. God was made flesh and lived among us. The eternal creator of all entered into history and lived the same life that we do. God was given a name and a story to tell, and a life to try and live well. God walks with us not in majesty, but in the ordinariness and overwhelming fleshliness of our lives.

The Poor Child of Bethlehem

The custom of setting up a nativity scene at Christmas, which seems to most of us today so central to the liturgical celebration of the season, is a relatively new custom in Christian practice. Francis of Assisi, the thirteenth century Italian holy man whom most Americans know mainly as a picturesque saint who loved animals and sang to the sun and moon, is credited with initiating the practice of erecting the Christian crib. He, more clearly than most of us, saw the baby in the manger as a sign of divine affection for our intrinsic poverty.

Francis is one of the most remarkable of figures in the annals of our religious heritage, a much richer and more complex man than his concrete garden birdbath image would suggest. Francis was a man madly in love with God. The eldest son of a wealthy cloth merchant, Francis grew up, boisterous and adventuresome, in the lap of medieval urban middle class comfort. Like many of his young companions, Francis coveted the glory of a solder's life and so set out to serve in the forces of a neighboring nobleman. After a brief term of service, which included time spent as a prisoner, the ebullient young man had a dream in which he saw his father's house was transformed into a castle decorated with armor marked with the cross. A voice informed him the armor belonged to him. Confident of his knightly future, the next day Francis set off into battle but, to his dismay, fell gravely ill. Lying in bed, he realized that his real call was to serve the great Lord, not the lesser one. He was to enlist in the service of the Lord Christ. Rapidly, the young man's life began to change. He exchanged his elegant clothing for simple garb, and began to experience identity with the poorest and most despised of the citizenry. Riding one day on the plains below Assisi he caught sight of a leper whose running sores filled him with horror. Leaping off his horse, he ran to give the leper his money and then kissed his ulcerated hand. From that day on, Francis was wed to his love, Lady Poverty, as he called her.

Responding to another divinely-authored dream, Francis sold some of his father's cloth goods so that he might give the money for the repair of a nearby dilapidated church. Furious, his father hauled him into the public square before the bishop and demanded restitution. Francis returned the money, but then proceeded to strip off his clothing and present it to his father, declaring that from that moment on he would call no one father but "Our Father, who art in Heaven." Now cut off from all previous ties, he embarked on a new life that fueled the gossip throughout the region. He roamed the highways, singing God's praise and, with a small band of companions, attempted to live out the exhortation of Matthew 10:7-19: "Go, preach, saying the kingdom of God is at hand . . . take neither gold nor silver nor brass in your purses . . . nor two coats nor shoes nor a staff." Many followed him, including a young noblewoman, Clare, who left the luxury and protection of her father's home to live an enclosed life of prayer and absolute poverty in solidarity with the ideal Francis lived in active form.

For Francis and Clare, to follow Christ was to be one who embraced poverty, both exterior and interior. To be a Christian was to imitate the cross-hung man who, through his intimate love of God, was stripped of everything. The saints from Assisi lived simply, without owning property, handling money, holding positions of influence, or acquiring great learning. They loved all that was simple, humble and unobtrusive. Especially they identified with the sufferings of the poor and marginalized, experiencing with them the kenotic destiny of the Lord they followed. One Christmas Eve, in the year 1223, Francis, now in mid-life and weary from the administrative conflicts that his numerous followers found themselves embroiled in, sought rest in the little village of Greccio. Wishing to reflect, in his distinctively literal way, on the nature of the child whose birth was celebrated that night, Francis asked that a crude stable with live animals and a newborn child be set up in the hermitage where he was staying. He wished to behold with his own eyes the hardships of the child born in Bethlehem, to vividly see the poverty of Christ, the poor man who emptied himself and became one of us.

That spontaneous Franciscan tableau in the hermitage at Greccio was the beginning of the custom of the Christmas crib. It was to be a visual reminder of the unspeakable humility of God become human, of the stark poverty of life lived in imitation of Christ, of the vulnerability of a heart stripped of everything but God.

Certainly the concept of the poverty of the Christ-event as seen at the moment of the incarnation resides deep in the Christian spiritual tradition. For centuries, monastic life, which was understood to be a school for the Lord's service, espoused poverty as one of its main vows. From earliest times, selling all one had and giving it to the poor was seen as a prerequisite for serious discipleship. This literal action was symbolic of entry into a deeper ontological reality expressed in the image of divinity so impoverished that it was limited by humanity's finite state. Christians celebrated this mystery from the earliest years. Ephrem the Syrian, the greatest Christian poet of the fourth century church, brought his creative genius eloquently to bear upon this mystery of the incarnation in his *Hymns on the Nativity*.

> Blessed be the Child Who today delights Bethlehem.
> Blessed be the Newborn Who today made humanity young again.
> Blessed be the Fruit Who bowed Himself down for our   hunger.
> Blessed be the gracious One Who suddenly enriched all of our poverty and filled our need.
> Blessed be He Whose mercy inclined Him to heal our sickness.
> . . . . . .

On this night of the Humble One; let us be neither proud nor
   haughty.
On this day of forgiveness let us not avenge offenses.
On this day of rejoicings let us not share sorrows.
On this sweet day let us not be vehement.
On this calm day let us not be quick-tempered.
On this day on which God came into the presence of sinners
let not the just man exalt himself in his mind over the sinner.
On this day on which the Lord of all came among servants,
let the lords also bow down to their servants lovingly.
On this day when the Rich One was made poor for our sake,
let the rich man also make the poor man a sharer at his table.
On this day a gift came out to us without our asking for it;
let us then give alms to those who cry out and beg from us.
. . . . . .
In a manger
the Lord of the universe reclined for the sake of the universe.
. . . . . .
On this day our Lord exchanged
radiance for shame, as the Humble One.[46]

Ephrem the Syrian's rhapsodic hymnody reminds us that this
Feast of the Nativity is a liturgical window into the reality–half
shrouded in the night of uncreated life, half visible in the daylight of
created life–that divine and human are most intimately linked. They
are linked in the person of Jesus of Nazareth foremost, and in our own
persons as well. But this linkage only comes to fruition in us when we
enter into the cosmic dynamic imaged for us in the poor baby at
Bethlehem. God is conjoined to humankind through a radical kenosis.
So too we are conjoined to God through this same movement. As we
become poor, vulnerable, stripped of all the accumulations that clutter
our material and spiritual lives, we come close to the poverty of the
babe in the manger who, in adulthood, died ignominiously on a cross.

It is a striking and thought-provoking fact that two of the
central symbols of divinity found in our Christian religion are symbols
of profound poverty and vulnerability: the incarnation and the

crucifixion. The poverty that these symbols refract for us is many faceted. Always, it is a challenge to our unreflected lives. What does it mean to be poor? Certainly it does not mean to glorify the degradation of involuntary poverty inflicted on so many in our world and nation in the present day. But it does mean something about our material wealth and about the just distribution of that wealth.

I have always been intrigued with the fact that at Christmas time Charles Dickens's little social novella, *A Christmas Carol,* is inevitably broadcast on airways across the United States. Several film versions of the story of mean tight-fisted old Ebenezer Scrooge and his exploited but good-hearted worker, Bob Cratchit, and his heart-wrenching invalid boy Tiny Tim, replay themselves yearly. In Omaha, Nebraska, where we now live, the local community playhouse has a seasonal tradition of presenting the Dickens tale, which fills packed houses for much of the month of December. So popular is this production that the playhouse sponsors several different road show companies of the piece that travel throughout the country during the same time period. *A Christmas Carol* is a morality play about the spiritual desolation that comes with the hoarding of wealth and the inability to perceive the cries of the poor. In a terror-filled Christmas midnight dream miser Scrooge sees visions of Christmas past, present, and future, revealing the joyful past promises of his life thrown away on the pursuit of money, the present cramped and endangered state of his soul and the horrors of a future of perpetual enslavement in the chains of his own selfishness and greed. How theater audiences love it when Scrooge, having had the veil of his own blindness torn away, shows up at the house of the impoverished Cratchit family bearing a fattened goose and toys and promises of medical help for sickly Tiny Tim. Somehow we know that Christmas is about the just distribution of resources, about the cries of the poor, and about our own responsibility to hear and respond to them.

But there are other facets of Christmas time poverty as well. For Francis and Clare, imitation of the poor Christ was not exhausted by walking barefoot and owning only one cloak. It also meant poverty of spirit. Sometimes it seems we shrink from notions like poverty of spirit because we see only the negative, dehumanizing face of poverty around us. We should, rightfully, recoil at a spirituality that would hold up self-loathing or victimization as an ideal. But poverty of spirit does not refer primarily to this. It refers to a freedom of spirit, an inner life unencumbered by excessive psychological baggage.

What inner poverty is genuinely about is loving well. It is about intimacy. Francis and Clare and other great lovers in the tradition knew that true intimacy with God and others means allowing oneself to know and be known. It means letting down the barriers of self defense that separate us. It means becoming unselfconsciously naked, so that we might joyfully enter into true intimacy with another. The poverty of the babe in the manger is the poverty of a heart simple enough to let itself be seen in its utter vulnerability, open enough to let itself be touched and changed by the encounter with love.

Christmas time, as a season of the spirit, is a time of tender poverty when, in our weaknesses, we allow ourselves to ask for and receive love. It is a time for recognizing our needfulness for one another and for God. It is a moment when we are urged to gentle ourselves, to become seekers of intimacy in the truest sense. For our desires to know and be known are far deeper than the desire for physical intimacy. We long for emotional, intellectual, and, especially, spiritual intimacy as well. Encoded in the structure of the human person is the desire to return home to the divine source, to become one with God. The more we free ourselves from our needless preoccupation with acquiring wealth, position, prestige, or power beyond the satisfaction of basic human needs, the poorer we are. Thus, the more willing recipients we will be of God's love that so yearns to enfold us, and the better we will be able to accept the love of family and friends.

The poverty of Christmas is the emptiness of our poverty filled to overflowing with the beneficence of the divine gift giver. It is truly a season in which to sing with Clare of Assisi:

> O blessed poverty,
> who bestows eternal riches
> on those who love and embrace her!
> O holy poverty,
> to those who possess and desire you
> God promises the kingdom of heaven
> And offers, indeed, eternal glory and blessed life!
> O God-centered poverty
> whom the Lord Jesus Christ
> Who ruled and now rules heaven and earth,
> Who spoke and things were made,
> condescended to embrace before all else.

. . . If so great and good a Lord, then, on coming into the Virgin's womb, chose to appear despised, needy, and poor in this world, so that people who were in utter poverty and want and in absolute need of heavenly nourishment might become rich in Him by possessing the kingdom of heaven, then rejoice and be glad! Be filled with a remarkable happiness and a spiritual joy![47]

God-With-Us

ONE OF MY FAVORITE VISUAL INTERPRETATIONS of the Annunciation—the announcement of God's messenger, Gabriel, to the astonished young woman Mary that she was to bear a child—is a fresco done by the fifteenth century Florentine artist, Fra Angelico. A Dominican monk, Fra Angelico gave expression to his life of prayerful divine intimacy by covering the walls of his monastery with visual portrayals of the stories of faith. In his *Annunciation* Fra Angelico locates Mary and her angelic visitor in a bare, arched portico. Each of the figures which face one another on opposite sides of the composition lean slightly forward, recapitulating the overhanging arch of the cell. The fresco's primary hues range from light brown to sand to pale pink and rose. The two principles of the scene, in the artist's distinctive style, are exquisitely drawn. Tender and fragile-featured, they nonetheless radiate a sense of spiritual graciousness and depth. The young woman sits upon a low bench, her arms clasped across her breast, her head bowed slightly as if she had just received news that took her breath away. Gabriel stands at a respectful distance, an equally gentle figure, the calm repose of his wings and the drapes of his garment suggesting the reverence with which he has entered upon the scene. His hands too are clasped before him and he looks slightly down upon the young woman with a direct yet tender gaze. The artist gives to us a vision of this moment distilled from the fruits of his contemplative prayer.

Sometime during the cycle of this season we will have heard proclaimed the familiar words of the first chapter of Luke:

> In the sixth month the angel Gabriel was sent by God to a town in Galilee called Nazareth, to a virgin betrothed to a man named Joseph, of the House of David; and the virgin's name was Mary. He went in and said to her, 'Rejoice, so highly favored! The

Lord is with you.' She was deeply disturbed by these words and asked herself what this greeting could mean, but the angel said to her, 'Mary do not be afraid; you have won God's favour. Listen! You are to conceive and bear a son, and you must name him Jesus. He will be great and will be called Son of the Most High. The Lord God will give him the throne of his ancestor David; he will rule over the House of Jacob forever and his reign will have no end.' Mary said to the angel, 'But how can this come about, since I am a virgin?' 'The Holy Spirit will come upon you,' the angel answered, 'and the power of the Most High will cover you with its shadow. And so the child will be holy and will be called Son of God. Know this too: your kinswoman Elizabeth has, in her old age, herself conceived a son, and she whom people called barren is now in her sixth month, for nothing is impossible with God.' 'I am the handmaid of the Lord,' said Mary 'let what you have said be done to me.' And the angel left her.[48]

This scriptural moment, understood in tradition as the moment when the Spirit of God descended and came to dwell in humankind, has been treasured over the centuries as one of the richest and most meaningful truths of the Christian revelation. Mary is seen not simply as an historical personage, the young Jewish wife of Joseph, who was the Mother of Jesus. She is also, in the shared understanding of our heritage, the archetype of all humankind. She is humanity responding to the breath of the Spirit, assenting to the indwelling of God. Contemplatives at prayer for centuries have gazed upon the posture and the words of Mary at the Annunciation to discern there the attitude characteristics of such assent. For it was assumed that this scriptural passage was multivalent. It referred, on the one hand, to a one-time event, which gives us a glimpse into a salvific mystery that was concretely located in place and time in Palestine two thousand years ago. Tradition also assumed that the indwelling of the Spirit was a continuing occurrence taking place within the hearts and minds of Christians in each age. Like Mary, each individual was visited by the divine Spirit who bore an invitation: to become the dwelling place of Christ. Each woman or man was invited to become a Mother of God.

It was the medieval Cistercian tradition that gave especially eloquent articulation to this idea. The men and women of this monastic order, which had its origins in twelfth century France, found much food for reflection in the mystery of the incarnation and dwelt lovingly on the scriptural images and feasts expressive of that mystery: Advent, Christmas, Epiphany, the purification, and the circumcision. They took seriously the Pauline notion that the Christian life was to be a new life in which "I now no longer live but Christ lives in me" (Galatians 2:20). Prominent in their thought was the idea that in the church the fullness of life promised by Jesus becomes realized. In the Spirit-filled life of the Christian community, humanity comes to maturity in divinity. Each member of the church, the mystical body, participates in this continual and continuous filling out of the Christ-event. The twelfth century was an era of vital Christian humanism. As such, its theological reflection proceeded, as it were, from the underside. It was preoccupied with human experience (especially in its spiritual dimension), and from that vantage point arose reflection upon divine life. The age took seriously the claim that the Spirit of Christ dwells in and vitalizes the life of the church and its members.

When Cistercian authors, most of whom were writing or preaching for their monastic contemporaries who were assumed to be about the business of the spiritual (i.e. Spirit-filled) life in earnest, spoke of the Annunciation, they saw themselves in Mary. She was the one they were to imitate if they too were to become bearers of the Spirit and Mothers of God. Cistercian interpretations of the scriptural imagery reveal the profound psychological and spiritual insight of these medieval writers and preachers. Guerric of Igny, when meditating on the Annunciation, emphasized the spiritual maturity imaged in the person of Mary that is the vocation of each spiritually vital member of the body of Christ.

> Now that you may know more fully that the Virgin's conception has not only a mystical but also a moral sense, what is a mystery for your redemption is also an example of your imitation, so that you clearly frustrate the grace of the mystery in you if you do not imitate the virtue of the example. For she who conceived God by faith promises you the same if you have faith; if you will faithfully receive the Word from the mouth of the heavenly messenger you too may conceive the God whom the whole world cannot contain, conceive him however in your heart, not in your body. And yet even in your body, although not by any bodily action or outward form, nonetheless truly in your body, since the Apostle bids us glorify and bear God in our body. He who created you is created in you, and as if it were too little that you should possess the Father, he wishes also that you should become a mother to himself. "Whoever," he says, "does the will of my Father he is my brother and sister and mother." O faithful soul, open wide your bosom, expand your affections, admit no constraint in your heart, conceive him whom creation cannot contain. Open to the Word of God an ear that will listen. This is the way to the womb of your heart for the Spirit who brings about conception; in such fashion are the bones of Christ, that is the virtues, built up in pregnant womb.[49]

Like Mary, we open to the Word. Like Mary, we gestate and give birth to the Word through the actions of our lives. Like Mary, we are involved in the process of bringing God into the world. Like Mary, we are the finite earthen vessels into which infinite divine life is poured. Guerric of Igny, in playful fashion, drew out his metaphor and thus underscored the notion that our participation in this God-bearing is neither negligible nor passive.

Rather, we are active recipients, persons whose freedom of choice is never violated. The request that we allow the dynamics of divinity to be realized through the medium of our lives is a genuine one. We can refuse. Or we can assent and let the most intimate recesses of our lives be inhabited, transformed, made new by God. But the divine action is neither mechanical nor invasive. It requires our conscious cooperation. We must nurture the Spirit into maturity in our lives.

> Thanks be to you, Spirit, who breathe where you will. By your gift I see not one but countless faithful souls pregnant with that noble offspring. Preserve your works, lest anyone should suffer miscarriage and expel, shapeless and dead, the progeny he has conceived of God.
>
> You also, blessed mothers of so glorious an issue, attend to yourselves until Christ is formed in you. Be careful lest any violent blow coming from without should injure the tender foetus, lest you should take into your stomach, that is your mind, anything which might extinguish the spirit you have conceived. Spare, if not yourselves, at least the Son of God in you; spare him not only from evil deeds and utterances but also from harmful thoughts and deadly pleasures which obviously stifle the seed of God. You have conceived the spirit of salvation, but you are still in labor, you have not yet given birth. If there is labor in giving birth, great consolation comes from the hope of offspring. A woman in childbirth feels the distress of labor; but when she has borne her child she will not remember the distress any longer, so glad will she be that a man, Christ, has been born into the outer world of our body, which is accustomed to be called a world in miniature.[50]

This insight, common to the medieval contemplative tradition, that the physical motherhood of Mary is recapitulated in the spiritual Motherhood to which all Christians are heir, re-echoes down the centuries and finds poetic articulation through Gerard Manley Hopkins in nineteenth century England. In the densely textured "The Blessed Virgin Compared to the Air We Breathe," Hopkins gives voice to the same astounding insight: that we are Mothers of God.

Of her flesh he took flesh:
He does take fresh and fresh,
Though much the mystery how,
Not flesh but spirit now.
And makes, O marvelous!
New Nazareths in us,
Where she shall yet conceive
Him, morning, noon, and eve;
New Bethlems, and he born.
There, evening, noon, and morn.[51]

Opening to God

God is with us! This is the proclamation made visible to us in the brightness of Christmas Day. We are radically accompanied. There is nothing in human experience that is not touched and ultimately transfigured by divine life itself. Matter is suffused with spirit. We are not alone. God walks with us as friend, as sharer in our finite existence. The promises heard through the mouth of the prophet Isaiah take on flesh. We enter into the new reality which ushers us into the final fulfillment of the promises hidden in the heart of God: Unto us a child is born!

For much of her history, the church sensed that the birth of the baby in the manger in Bethlehem was the wondrous beginning of a greater unfolding mystery held close in the desire of God. Today, the common lectionary for the second reading on Christmas Day is the second chapter of Paul's letter to Titus which enlarges our focus on the first coming of Christ to include the second coming.

> You see, God's grace has been revealed, and it has made salvation possible for the whole human race and taught us that what we have to do is give up everything that does not lead to God, and all our worldly ambitions; we must be self-restrained and live good and religious lives here in this present world, while we are waiting in hope for the blessing which will come with the

Appearing of the glory of our great God and Saviour Christ Jesus.[52]

We, as persons baptized in the waters of new birth in Christ, fully participate in the unfolding mystery that has its culmination at the Second Coming. As imitators of Mary in our spiritual maternity, medieval commentators saw us as engaged in a cosmic drama whose full story would not be known until the end of time. Until then we were lovingly invited, wooed even, to open our lives to the dynamic activity of the Spirit acting to bring about the fullness of God's plan.

The cosmic drama is one in which Christians of all generations have been schooled. The first act of the drama, as most commentators would have it, began with creation itself, proceeded with the fall of humankind (in Adam), and redemption (in Christ's crucifixion and resurrection) and would conclude with the Second Coming. The redemptive moment of the incarnation was understood in a variety of ways depending on the era and commentator, but one of the earliest Christian attempts at imaging the transition from one state to another that redemption implies was the image of Christ as the Second Adam. Patristic writers saw in the incarnation a transformation of the human condition. Christ reversed the fall of Adam, thus redeeming humankind. But the story included other principal characters. Just as, according to the exegesis of the time, Eve was instigator of Adam's fall, so another woman, Mary, was essential to its reversal. In Mary's assent, her responsive welcome of God's desire for the world, she allowed the transformation of the human condition to occur.

Medieval contemplative writers applied the cosmic imagery of the Second Adam and Second Eve scenario to the redemptive drama going on within the individual soul. Thus, particular attitudes or spiritual tempers came to be seen as mirroring the attitude of Mary. She was open, responsive, and assenting. So important to generations of commentators was the spiritual opening that we accomplish that they, with painstaking attention, turned the words and the image of the Annunciation over and over to reflect all the spiritual illumination contained there. For many, it was Mary as the chosen spouse of God that was the focus of reflection. Mary as bride became the archetype for the loving soul seeking union with the divine spouse. The use of nuptial language to speak of the relationship between God and humankind goes back, of course, to the Hebrew roots of revelation. The covenant between God and God's chosen people, Israel, was long elaborated with bridal imagery, and that imagery was adopted by the church. God was spouse, the church the beloved bride. The analogy was extended to refer to God and the Virgin Mary as well as to God and the individual soul. All were relationships captured in the language of mutual desire, faithfulness, and fruitful love.

Especially in the high middle ages the imagery of contemplative prayer was permeated with nuptial symbolism. The biblical book, *The Song of Songs,* which depicts the mutual search of desire between a man and woman, was frequently alluded to in monastic preaching and literature. Mary, as spouse, wholly oriented toward her beloved, was the model for the praying soul giving single-focused attention to God. Mary's virginity, which spoke of her belonging solely to her divine spouse, was a frequent topic of concern. Like the soul "married" to God alone, Mary was both virgin and fruitful. With passionate imagination medieval religious writers teased out the implications of the betrothal between the human and divine depicted in the Annunciation.

One of the most original of these voices, Hildegard of Bingen, twelfth century abbess of the Benedictine monastery of Rupertsberg in the Rhineland, composed hymns and sequences that celebrated the virgin (God-focused) fecundity of the Virgin Mary, and thus the individual soul. Hildegard's frankly erotic language heightens the spousal metaphor so strikingly elaborated in her "Ave Generosa."

Hail, great-souled, renowned, and innocent maid!
You are the artless apple of God's eye;
the embodiment of holiness pleasing to God are you.

For to you came this heavenly outpouring:
heaven's Word took flesh in you.

The bright lily that God gazed upon
before the world was made is you.
Most lovely and winning of women,
God took as much delight in you
when he put his arms of ardor around you
as his Son did when he drew from you his milk.

Indeed, Virgin, your womb rejoiced
when all the choirs of heaven
sang of you, that within your chastity
resplendent in God, you bore God's Son.

Your womb rejoiced
as grass does when the dew
falling on it fills it with fruitfulness—
as happened in you, Mother of all joy.

Let the church now glow in its joy
and celebrate in song
the Virgin most winning,
the praiseworthy Mary, mother of God.[53]

Not only was the spousal fidelity and surrender to God imaged
in the Annunciation seen as a spiritual attitude to be emulated, the
profound openness and receptivity captured there were to be imitated
as well. Bernard of Clairvaux, Hildegard's contemporary and
correspondent who was the guiding light of the Cistercian reform,
wrote frequently of the virtue of humility—best translated perhaps as
openness or receptivity—that creates in the person an empty space
where the Spirit can indwell. For Bernard and others like him, God-

with-us is most truly realized when we open ourselves in contemplative readiness to be entered by the Word of God. Then the Word takes on flesh in the leanings of our hearts and the actions of our lives. The indwelling of the Christ-life rightly engenders in us profound humility. It is not a false humility which focuses solely on its own unworthiness, but the true humility of a person aware of containing within herself that which cannot be contained, a creature awed that he bears within himself his creator.

Eight centuries later, English devotional writer Caryll Houselander picks up the identical theme in her volume *Reed of God.*

> That virginal quality which, for want of a better word, I call emptiness is the beginning of this contemplation.
>
> It is not a formless emptiness, a void without meaning; on the contrary it has a shape, a form given to it by the purpose for which it is intended.
>
> It is emptiness like a hollow in the reed, the narrow riftless emptiness which can have only one destiny: to receive the piper's breath and to utter the song that is in his heart.
>
> It is the emptiness like the hollow in the cup, shaped to receive water or wine.
>
> It is emptiness like that of the bird's nest, built in a round warm ring to receive the little bird.
>
> The pre-Advent emptiness of Our Lady's purposeful virginity was indeed like those three things.
>
> She was a reed through which the Eternal Love was to be piped as a shepherd's song. . . .
>
> God had taken his little reed into his hands and the breath of His love sang through it, and this utterance would go on for all generations. . . .
>
> In surrendering to the Spirit and becoming the Bride of Life, she wed God to the human race and made the whole world pregnant with the life of Christ. . . .
>
> She had given mankind the key. Indeed, she had unlocked and opened the door of every heart. Now men had only to leave it open.[54]

God Between Us

In his brief meditative treatise on this Annunciation mystery of God-with-us, *Bringing Forth Christ*, Bonaventure, a thirteenth century Franciscan theologian, observed that according to scripture, after conceiving the Spirit of God, Mary went up to the hill country to visit her cousin Elizabeth. Because, he commented:

> After this conception . . . the soul begins to flee the company of those *with minds set on earthly things* (Phil. 3:19) and desires the friendship of those with hearts set on heavenly things. It begins to take care of Elizabeth, that is, to look to those who are enlightened by divine wisdom and ardently enflamed by love.[55]

What Bonaventure points to here is a truth central to the Christmastide proclamation that God is with us. Not only do we realize that God dwelt among us in the humanity of Jesus, not only do we know that divinity is now present in humanity, not only do we experience God-with-us in the Spirit acting in the church, not only do we wait for our final "at-one-ment" with God, not only do we receive the Spirit in the depths of our beings as we open ourselves to be vessels of the living Word—we also come to know that God is with us "in the in-between," that God's presence is discovered in the zestful, life-giving relationships that we cultivate.

As the light of Christmas Day radiates around us, we would do well to turn our attention to those with whom we live the miracle of God-with-us—spouses, children, parents, in-laws, church members, colleagues, neighbors, small group participants, pastors, mentors, guides, friends. We do not live it alone. As intently personal as the encounter with God in the depths of our hearts might be, it is never essentially private. For in the most intimate recesses of our beings, where we open out to the Spirit's call, we are most deeply connected to one another. God is with us and we are with one another.

This is a time to access and celebrate our relationships. Who are the persons God has entrusted to me? Are my interactions with these persons expressive of the Christ-life that I am called to bring into the world? And, equally important, am I being nurtured in the Christ-life by these persons? Our destiny to become mothers of God does not take place in a psychic and spiritual vacuum. Just as a new biological mother finds support and nurture for her changing identity in the circle of friends and loved ones who care for and encourage her, so spiritual maternity calls for the support of a caring community as well.

I was recently invited to a house-blessing party by a single woman in the community where we live. She was a woman who was growing rich in her own sense of calling—the calling to respond generously with her gifts and to enter into deeper intimacy with God in prayer. The blessing of her first house was significant, for it symbolized her own conscious embrace of the idea that the single life is a specific Christian vocation, not simply a temporary stopping point on the way to being married or to living in vowed religious life. Neither was it an unasked for alternative for the no-longer-married, the no-longer-in community, the never-been-married, or the never-been-vowed.

She invited the circle of persons who were, for her, significant in her own journey home to God. Mainly they were part of an on-going faith sharing group that met monthly to break bread and break open the hard crusts of their lives so that God might enter and be seen there. But there were others at the party as well—parish members, her pastor, her spiritual director. During the actual blessing ceremony, she darkened the house and then invited us to light the candles she had requested we bring. After blessing the living room together, we each went to a doorway of the house's respective rooms. She then moved from room to room with the officiant of the blessing and, as each room was blessed, those who stood at that doorway placed their candles within the room. The light from the flickering wicks illuminated the dark, reflecting the unique presence of each visitor somewhere within the house. The light symbolized the light of Christ coming to indwell in each facet of this woman's life, the presence of the Spirit vitalizing each aspect of her day. And the light was placed there by others who share her faith. For me, this simple house blessing illumined again the truth that God comes to dwell in us through the medium of other people.

We all need companions on the way. We thrive best in concentric and ever-widening circles of care. This has always been the assertion of the church: that we need one another to know and grow into God. That is what Christian community ideally is about. Unfortunately, the congregations or parishes in which people find themselves are not always supportive environments in which to find compassionate guidance and vital companionship in the life of faith. Often we must look to small faith sharing groups, renewal movements, retreat experiences, and individual spiritual guidance to find such enlivening interaction. But seek we must. And, if we are serious about the mystery of God-with-us, we must be willing to be companions for others too.

Our accompaniment goes much deeper than simply acknowledgment of one another or even faith sharing. While telling our stories and listening to one another's stories and allowing those stories to be gradually woven into the fabric of the greater faith story that encompasses our little lives is an essential part of nurturing the Christ-life within, it cannot stop there. We must become sensitive to the true nature of our connectedness. We are all children of God. Our origin and end is the same. In each of our hearts is planted the seed of desire to draw nearer Godward. As we come to discover that restless yearning within ourselves, we begin to identify it in the longings of others. Soon we perceive that our desire, when shared, is enlivened and enflamed. The mutual exchange of love between persons gives birth to God in and between us. Luke tells us that:

> Mary set out at that time and went as quickly as she could to a town in the hill country of Judah. She went into Zechariah's house and greeted Elizabeth. Now as soon as Elizabeth heard Mary's greeting, the child leapt in her womb and Elizabeth was filled with the Holy Spirit. She gave a loud cry and said, 'Of all women you are the most blessed, and blessed is the fruit of your womb. Why should I be honoured with a visit from the mother of my Lord? For the moment your greeting reached my ears, the child in my womb leapt for joy. Yes, blessed is she who believed that the promise made her by the Lord would be fulfilled.' [56]

The relational mystery of this moment of the "Visitation" has not escaped the eye of spiritual commentators. The inner resonance, the shared recognition, the mutual awe and delight of these two women, Mary and Elizabeth, has often served as a reminder that we bear Christ to one another and that in our interaction the Spirit is called down and vitalizes us. Something of the marvel that earlier Christians have felt in this scriptural tableau is exuberantly captured by Jeremy Taylor, the seventeenth century Anglican divine.

> It is not easy to imagine what a collision of joys was at this blessed meeting: two mothers of two great princes, the one the greatest that was born of woman, and the other was his Lord, and these made mothers by two miracles, met together with joy and mysteriousness; where the mother of our Lord went to visit the mother of His servant, and the Holy Ghost made the meeting festival, and descended upon Elizabeth, and she prophesied. Never, but in heaven, was there more joy and ecstasy: the persons, who were women whose fancies and affections were not only hallowed, but made pregnant and big with religion, meeting together to compare and unite their joys and their eucharist, and then made prophetical and inspired, must needs have discoursed like seraphims and the most ecstasied order of intelligences; for all the faculties of nature were

turned into grace, and expressed in their way the excellent solemnity: "for it came to pass, when Elizabeth heard the salutation of Mary, the babe leaped in her womb; and Elizabeth was filled with the Holy Ghost." [57]

A collision of joys. What a delightfully worded phrase to express the feeling of the meeting of two hearts that carry God to one another, and how appropriate is the image of two pregnant women. For there *is* a secret communion between women who literally hold new life within them, a curious shared wonder exchanged in a passing glance. Taylor says it well–a collision of joys that transcends race, creed, age, or background. There is a pregnant knowing that viscerally experiences the incomprehensible actuality of new life. Women ripe to bursting know it in the shortness of their breath, the weight of their bodies, and the increased coursing of their blood. All of us know the origin of this pregnant truth somewhere deep within, for we are all potentially vessels of new life.

We know it primarily through the yearning of our hearts, through our desire to be touched and touch one another at the level of the heart where we intersect with God. We recognize our potential in one another. We actuate that potential through the vital, life-giving communion that goes on between us. We form each other's hearts by making them pliant and enlarging their contours. Our visitations to each other are never simply routine, they are pregnant. For God is with us through the medium of our enfleshed lives. Might we cry out, like Elizabeth, in astonishment and joy, as God's presence within is stirred to life in our meetings with each other?

LIVING THE SEASON

You are utterly a wonder. In every side that we seek You,
You are near and far, but who is it that reaches You?
Investigation is not able to stretch it[self] to reach You.
Whenever it stretches out to reach [You],
   it is cut off and falls short.
It is too short for Your mountain. Faith reaches [You]
   —and love and prayer.

The Magi, too, sought Him,
   and when they found Him in the crib,
worship instead of investigation they offered Him in silence.
Instead of empty controversies, they gave Him offerings.
You, too, seek the First-born, and if you find Him on high,
   instead of confused searchings,
         open your treasures before him
   and offer Him your deeds.[58]

EPHREM THE SYRIAN
(Fourth Century)

Dark

THE CHURCH DOES NOT abandon the celebration of Christmas on December twenty-sixth. Liturgically, the season stretches out for twelve more days and culminates on the Feast of Epiphany, January sixth.[59] In earlier days, in England, these days were kept as a time of merriment during which ancient customs, such as lighting twelve bonfires for the twelve apostles, were observed. It was also a time of gift-giving; the familiar carol, "The Twelve Days of Christmas," regales modern carolers with the antics of an eighteenth-century merrymaker who sent his true love a veritable barnyard and theater company of presents as well as a partridge in a pear tree. (The French version of the song, sung across the English Channel in the same century, has the gormandizing lover sending breasts of veal, legs of mutton, spitted rabbits, plates of salad, beautiful full-breasted maidens and musketeers with their swords.)

Our commercially oriented American society has little room for this kind of delightful, fanciful lingering over a season. Christmas comes to a screeching halt for us the day after. The only vestiges of merriment are found in the after-Christmas sales, where opportunistic shoppers can be found rummaging through bins of marked down merchandise that only a few days before radiated the possibility of being the answer to someone's Christmas gift wish. The frenzy of holiday partying subsides, and Americans begin to look with grim determination toward the fashioning of New Year's resolutions to lose those accumulated pounds, kick that pernicious habit, or do something better.

That the season is over, in the secular public arena, is obvious from the fact that store decorations quickly disappear and the spate of holiday specials broadcast on television are suddenly eclipsed by re-runs of old movies and last year's serials. Even in the domestic realm, the vestiges of the season vanish. I am always startled to see how many upended Christmas trees, tinsel clinging to their stiff, twisted branches, top the piles of debris set out on the sidewalks for the city sanitary engineers to take away on December twenty-sixth.

I personally often suffer a mild sort of postpartum depression the day after the Coming itself. All the anticipation of the waiting and the heightened experience of the birth day itself are now memories, and we are left with the miracle in our arms and the overwhelming sensation that we have only just been initiated into the truth of it: that we are called to nurture and raise to maturity what has been given. We become aware that we must live, as well as anticipate, the Coming.

Most churches stubbornly resist the cultural amnesia that pervades the atmosphere and keep reminding us, through the proclamation of the word, the images of the Christmas crib, and the melodies of the songs of the season, that Christmas is still very much with us. And many homes stay decorated with signs of the wondrous birth. I have never been able to take our tree down until after Epiphany, even when brittle needles litter the floor, and the presents that blossomed under it have long since been put away. For the days following the Feast of the Nativity are rich in insight and wisdom. They are the days when we contemplate the Christ given to us, the days when the great task of living into the reality of our spiritual maternity is ours to ponder. They are, in some sense, not unlike the first days home after the trip to the hospital, or the time after the midwife or the last helpful female relative leaves you, at last, on your own. You are faced with both the wonderful, frustrating, impenetrable joy and the anxiety-filled responsibility of attending to new life.

In the Roman communion the Sunday after Christmas is always dedicated to the Holy Family, and for a liturgical moment we get a glimpse beyond the crib of the long ago family of three, busy about the work of nurturing, providing, and domestic labor. I have always felt somewhat ambivalent about this feast, in part because a saccharine mid-century piety still sometimes clings to its observance. Homilies I most remember from years past include, first, a nostalgic tale about a large family of boys whose father always insisted on an hour of quiet after supper, during which the preacher as a young man learned the value of self discipline; and second, a moralizing admonition about how Joseph certainly would not have gone out on New Year's Eve and had too many cocktails and gotten in his car to drive home. During this last exhortation, I remember futilely stretching my imagination to envision a first century Palestinian Jew entering a New York night club for a martini or counting down the last seconds of the old year ready to break into an Aramaic "Auld Lang Syne." In part the celebration is puzzling to me because we tend to so idealize the Holy Family that it practically becomes a barrier to celebrating our own familied lives. We conceive of them as *so* ideal, *so* untouched by the frustrations and banality of our experience, that they can become the source of feelings of self-condemnation and inadequacy. We make Mary into the perfect mother, Joseph the ideal protective father figure, Jesus into the model child. Then we are let down and discouraged when we turn our attention to our own lived reality.

The delight with which my children enter into the anticipation of Christmas always seems to sour in the let-down of the first days afterward. Perhaps this is partly because of our culture's excessive materialism. When the excitement of making out Christmas gift lists and waiting up for Santa is done, there is little lingering delight. The toys that were such objects of yearning are soon found broken or overlooked in the heap of post-holiday debris. Even if we try to minimize the omnipresent emphasis on acquisition and focus on the rich and unchanging qualities of the season, the disappointment is there in other ways. Our families are hardly the image of our dream of the Holy Family. The tedium of returning to work and its burdens soon clouds our spouse's festive mood. We find ourselves glad that in-laws have gone home. Somebody's aunt is always a trial at Christmas dinner or a painful feud leaves a place conspicuously empty at the family table. Perhaps a recent death or divorce spreads its blanket of sorrow about the circle of family gathered around the tree. The kids get bored of vacation and begin to bicker, and teenagers soon are negotiating for more cash to alleviate their pent-up up emotions at the after Christmas sales at the mall.

At such times, when the wonder and majesty of the season seems submerged in the vacuous and pain-filled realities of everyday life, I like to think of Joseph. Not as the idealized patriarch of the Holy Family, but as the overlooked figure in the Advent and Christmas story. My husband often has commented with irritation on the lack of an emulatable male model in the scripture readings this time of year. And he has been irked by the absence of human male generativity in the stories that get played out in our psyches seasonally. He wants to celebrate Joseph as more than an absentee father, more than the convenient payer of the bills and leader of the donkey, more than the provider of cribs, orthodontic work, and adequate schools. He would like to live into a Joseph who is deeply involved in the life of his family. While my husband can and does play out the scenarios of a generative Joseph in his own prayer with profit, it is quite hard to cull out from the gospel readings more than a shadowy, archetypal figure.

But it is precisely that shadowy Joseph who appeals to me at this particular point in the season. Joseph is the patient background of stability in front of which the life of the family is played out. Joseph represents for me the hidden, loving involvement in family, that comes from both men and women, that is neither obviously rewarding nor visible. Joseph is the innumerable sleepless nights tending a sick child, waiting up for a teen out on a date, or worrying over the placement of a failing parent in a rest home. Joseph is the countless "maintenance" meals cooked and sandwiched in between soccer games, ballet lessons, and PTA meetings. Joseph is taking in your sister and her kids as they suffer through a divorce. Joseph is the thousands of tiny moments of broken trust that get healed in a hug or an "I'm really sorry." Joseph is balancing the budget one more time, clipping out coupons, and reheating or disguising the leftovers in one more casserole surprise. Joseph is grieving with a parent slowly succumbing to Alzheimer's disease. Joseph is shouldering college tuition costs or giving Saturdays to coach the softball team. Joseph is all the endless, loving gestures of encouragement, the headache of defining appropriate guidelines, the challenge of keeping a meaningful conversation going with a spouse in the midst of it all. While I applaud my husband's creative efforts to reclaim a more dynamic Joseph viable for contemporary men, I also want to affirm Joseph's hidden life. For it is against this backdrop of stability and unflagging care, generated by both men and women, that the miracle of the divine birth is given a place to grow and mature in our families.

The Dark Side of the Season

For a few years, my annual post-Christmas slump was alleviated by the proximity of special friends. A couple we know, whose two boys are our godchildren, lived for several years in our immediate vicinity. Their first child was born in early December and they named him Stephen; so it was fitting that they should hold his baptism on the Feast of St. Stephen, which falls in the church calendar on the day after Christmas, the twenty-sixth. That year, and each year since, they have thrown a party, rich in religious symbolism, in honor of the saint and of their little boy. They have variously done dramatic readings of the daily scripture or renewed baptismal vows through the lighting of the baptismal candle that he received on his first St. Stephen's Day. At other times they have resuscitated the English custom of packing up gifts for the poor and distributing them (St. Stephen was a deacon, one of whose duties was to provide for the poor, so in England his feast day became known as "Boxing Day" for the boxing up of charitable gifts). Our friends have always remembered the feast with a mixture of gifts and reminders that, for some Christians like Stephen, the profession of faith has been serious business indeed. During the years that we lived nearby, we were always present at this familial gathering, and I welcomed this warm fellowship that continued to flesh out Christmastide.

The scripture readings for St. Stephen's Day contrast sharply with the mood of the scriptures we have attended to so far during the season. Generally, on the twenty-sixth, we listen to the word from Matthew and the Book of Acts. This latter reading from Acts 7 tells of Stephen, one of the first deacons selected for service in the nascent church in Jerusalem, whose preaching that the Spirit sent by Jesus transcended Mosaic Law did not endear him to the population.

> They were infuriated when they heard this, and ground their teeth at him. But Stephen, filled with the Holy Spirit, gazed into heaven and saw the glory of God, and Jesus standing at God's right hand. 'Look! I can see heaven thrown open,' he said, 'and the Son of Man standing at the right hand of God.' All the members of the council shouted out and stopped their ears with their hands; then they made a concerted rush at him, thrust him out of the city and stoned him. The witnesses put down their clothes at the feet of a young man called Saul. As they were stoning him, Stephen said in invocation, 'Lord, Jesus, receive my spirit.' Then he knelt down and said aloud, 'Lord, do not hold this sin against them.' And with these words he fell asleep.[60]*

This sobering account of the death of the first Christian martyr is underscored by the gospel reading of the day. In a particularly chilling prophetic passage in Matthew, Jesus is recorded as warning his disciples of the implications of discipleship.

> 'I am sending you out like sheep among wolves; so be cunning as snakes and yet innocent as doves. Be prepared for people to hand you over. . . . You will be universally hated on account of my name; but anyone who stands firm to the end will be saved.' [61*]

We are jarred, liturgically speaking, out of our tender and awestruck contemplation of the majesty and graciousness of God's love into the stark recognition that this Christian thing is not all sweetness. Instead, we are confronted with a sober message that there is likely to be a cost involved in our association with this man Jesus, the Christ. There is a foretaste of the passion even in the innocent season of the Nativity. The destiny of the vulnerable infant wrapped in swaddling clothes is foreshadowed, as is the destiny of all those who claim to follow in his path.

Only two days later on the church calendar, the Christian community observes another day of dark solemnity: the Feast of the Holy Innocents. December twenty-eighth commemorates the gripping drama narrated in the second chapter of the Gospel of Matthew. The evangelist tells us that after the birth of Jesus an angel appeared to Joseph in a dream and warned him that Herod, who was then King of Judea, was searching for the child in fear that he was destined to become a great ruler. Joseph was advised to take Mary and the child and to flee to Egypt to escape persecution until Herod's death. Herod, hoping to learn where this baby was to be found from foreign magi who were also seeking this child, was dismayed when the magi did not disclose the child's whereabouts to him.

> Herod was furious on realising he had been fooled by the wise men, and in Bethlehem and its surrounding district he had all the male children killed who were two years old and less, reckoning by the date he had been careful to ask the wise men.

Then were fulfilled the words spoken through the prophet Jeremiah:

> A voice is heard in Ramah,
> lamenting and weeping bitterly:
> it is Rachel weeping for her children,
> refusing to be comforted
> because they were no more.[62]*

This grisly scene, if truly prayed over, will chill the blood of any sensitive person. So soon we are reminded of the darkness present in the world into which the little child of Bethlehem comes. Yet this dark moment, as well as the feast of the first martyr Stephen, has been part of the Christian seasonal celebration for centuries. Late medieval guilds commonly presented religious dramas in the streets of European towns, each guild being responsible for enacting one "mystery" of the Christmas saga. From the fifteenth century Shearmen and Tailors Company at Coventry comes a carol composed for the mystery of the Slaying of the Innocents. We know it simply as the Coventry Carol. The song is sung by the women of Bethlehem just before Herod's soldiers come in to slaughter their children.

> *Lully, lullay, thou little tiny child*
> *By by, lully lullay:*
> *thou little tiny child*
> *By by, lully lullay.*

> *Herod, the king, In his raging,*
> *Charged he hath this day*
> *His men of might, In his own sight,*
> *All young children to slay.*

> *That woe is me, Poor child for thee*
> *And ever morn and day*
> *For thy parting Neither say nor sing*
> *By by, lully lullay.*

How marked is the contrast between these first days after Christmas and the days before. From such tenderness, hope, and beauty we are turned to sorrow and such necessity for suffering. Yet, if our embrace of the Christ child is to be authentic we must be aware that the world into which we bring him, while shot through with grace and presence, is also a world intractable in its resistance to God. So much of the way we live, as individuals, communities, and nations, has little room for such a gift. Despite our preparations and our efforts to make straight the highway for our God, we remain people of hilled and valleyed hearts.

How to celebrate this? One way, I would suggest, is to enter into the very dynamic that entered the world with the baby in the manger: the compassion of God. The birth of God in human form was not simply a gesture of divine attentiveness; it was a radical act of solidarity with the height and breadth of the human condition. God, in Jesus, suffered with us and probed the inner recesses of our darkness and pain. God-with-us. In everything, even the most seemingly God-less moments. God-with-us in our deaths and our dyings, our lostness, our despair, our brokenness, and our capacity for inflicting pain.

Perhaps we might celebrate the compassion of our ever present divine companion by being in solidarity with, suffering with, experiencing compassion with those who are suffering. There are some specifically seasonal ways to do this. One of the most unnoticed sufferings of the season is the quiet grief of persons for whom the holidays are not joy-filled times, but searing reminders of loss or unhappiness. My husband and I once were asked to lead a retreat called "The Christmas Extension" held annually at a California retreat house the week after Christmas. We were told that the people who tended to come to this gathering, whose theme was generally very loose and not particularly religious in orientation, were halves of broken families, widows or widowers, persons who had experienced some sort of loss or grief during the holiday season, surviving members of dwindling families, and persons estranged from their communities of support. Most of the retreatants wanted little structure from team leaders and a lot of time to simply be, a lot of space to wander in, some therapeutic things to do with their hands–clay work or paper cutting–and the freedom to either be with the other retreatants or not at any given time. The experience taught me a great deal about the dark power of the holiday season to rekindle painful memories and heighten awareness of the lack and the loss in our lives. It also taught me that the process of healing is long and that part of our gift to others or to ourselves in the post-Christmas days can be to provide a time for the natural course of grief to play itself out. It can be a time to allow ourselves to look into the darkened corners of our lives and become aware that, even there, we are not alone. Our God, who entered so utterly into our humanity, will walk with us no matter where our fragmented lives compel us to go. God is with us.

There is also a unique personal darkness each of us possesses and into which the Christ is born. We began our liturgical penetration of that darkness earlier in Advent, when we heard the fiery words of John the Baptist urging us to repent and straighten the crooked pathways of our lives. Hopefully we looked carefully at our habits and interactions at that time and resolved to enter into the slow, arduous effort of reform. Perhaps we resolved to discipline our prayer lives, or we decided to spend more time with our kids, or we have assessed our relationships and now refuse to be enablers in co-dependent situations, or we are taking better care of ourselves, or we are donating time at a local shelter for the homeless.

Yet even with these resolves, we discover that vast areas of personal darkness remain unchanged, and at this point in the season we find ourselves metaphorically treading water, struggling to move upstream against our own limitations. And, if you are anything like me, you very much want those limitations to not be there. With all the lofty aspirations of our spiritual longings, it is hard to be constantly brought back to earth and confronted with ourselves. But strangely, it is precisely our darkness that gives us a more penetrating glimpse into the mystery that we hold cradled in our arms. God is truly with us in everything. God's compassion and God's suffering with us really does reach into the depths where our own judgments, narrowness, and fears cannot plunge. We can never love ourselves with the wideness and mercy that God does. If, however, we are willing to look at and lovingly embrace our own limitations, we will begin to peer into the darkness and learn of the immensity of the love that awaits us there. "For God *so* loved the world . . . ."

But it takes our being compassionate with each other as well as being compassionate with ourselves. We must learn to love our limits, not simply recognize them (a challenging enough task in its own right). For it is precisely in our brokenness that we discover our need for God. It is in our weaknesses that we find we must reach out for one another. It is in our lack of vision that we are forced to search for light. And, as we venture tentatively into our darkness, holding fast to the hope that God has been there before us, we begin to view the immensity of the love that has been given to us. The American writer Annie Dillard has alluded to this strange paradox in *Teaching a Stone to Talk*, in which she describes our coming to know God. "You do not have to sit outside in the dark. If, however, you want to look at the stars, you will find that darkness is necessary." [63]

There is, likewise, a collective side to the face of darkness that we become aware of during the extended Christmas season. God's compassion reaches out mercifully into that collective darkness as well. Just as we are carried by the dynamic of divine compassion into the depths of our own sorrows and shortcomings, so we can be carried by that same momentum into the sorrows of the world.

In Omaha, where we now live, there is a different sort of ritual of seasonal solidarity that is enacted on December twenty-eighth each year, the Feast of the Holy Innocents. Local Christian justice and peace advocates sponsor a retreat day that focuses attention on the holy innocents of our own times. A diverse group of retreatants gather in the chilly winter weather to hear the proclamation of the word from Matthew. Then, after a day of prayerful reflection and some training in techniques of non-violent witness, participants are given a choice of sites at which to mount a public witness. Many choose the Strategic Air Command headquarters just south of the city. There, in protest of the policy of targeting nuclear warheads at millions of civilian children in the former Soviet Union, a peaceful prayer vigil is held. Other retreatants choose to wait in vigil at a local shelter for the homeless in solidarity with the growing numbers of children who now find themselves on the streets of America's cities at night. Other participants, who feel so moved, pray in front of an abortion clinic in witness to their belief that present day practices and the tragedy in Bethlehem two thousand years ago are analogous events.

It is not simply an act of political awareness to be in solidarity with the darkness that pervades our human communities. It is an act of spiritual awareness as well. For our Christian faith teaches us that God suffers with us, that in our dyings and in all that is covered by the shadow of death, we can discern the presence of a love that is, at the last, stronger than death itself. As the baby is born, the forces of darkness—fear, greed, and power—marshal to try to ferret out his hiding place and destroy him. As the Word is preached, the power of darkness—envy, rivalry, and bigotry—rises up to hunt down and stone the Word to death. This is the reality into which the infinitely overflowing love of God is prodigally poured. God suffers with us. But God's compassion cannot be bounded by the narrow confines of our lives. It spills over and seeps down into the farthest reaches of our pain. It wells up from the hidden ground waters of love that ultimately heal and sustain all creation. It bursts forth as newness and refreshment in the aridity of our lives. We can be carried in the current of that unbounded and ever present beauty.

To be in solidarity with suffering. To do as God did when divinity was intimately conjoined to humanity. To be compassion. To suffer with. This is the core of the dark beauty of the days after the birth. This is part of what it means to live the mystery of the Coming.

P e a c e

CHARLES WESLEY WHO, WITH HIS BROTHER JOHN, was the co-originator of the eighteenth century Methodist renewal movement within the Church of England, was one of Christianity's greatest hymn writers. His dramatic rendering of the scene portrayed in the second chapter of Luke rings out joyously so often in Christmas medleys during the holiday season. We know it as "Hark! the Herald Angels Sing."

> *Hark! the herald angels sing,*
> *"Glory to the newborn King;*
> *peace on earth, and mercy mild,*
> *God and sinners reconciled!"*
> *Joyful, all ye nations rise,*
> *join the triumph of the skies;*
> *With th' angelic host proclaim,*
> *"Christ is born in Bethlehem!"*
> *Hark! the herald angels sing,*
> *"Glory to the newborn King!"*
> *. . .*
> *Hail, the heaven-born Prince of Peace!*
> *Hail the Sun of Righteousness!*
> *Light and life to all he brings,*
> *risen with healing in his wings.*
> *Mild he lays his glory*
> *Born that we no more may die,*
> *Born to raise us from the earth,*
> *Born to give us second birth.*
> *Hark! The herald angels sing,*
> *"Glory to the newborn King!"*

Charles Wesley's musical setting of the angelic proclamation to the shepherds in the Judaean countryside heightens the drama and accentuates the majesty of the event. The bright staccatos of a brass quintet capture best the thrilling mood of Wesley's words, which elaborate upon and bring out the full Christological implications of the scriptural text.

> In the countryside close by there were shepherds who lived in the fields and took it in turns to watch their flocks during the night. The angel of the Lord appeared to them and the glory of the Lord shown round them. They were terrified, but the angel said, 'Do not be afraid. Listen, I bring you news of great joy, a joy to be shared by the whole people. Today in the town of David a saviour has been born to you; he is Christ the Lord. And here is a sign for you: you will find a baby wrapped in swaddling clothes and lying in a manger.' And suddenly with the angel there was a great throng of the heavenly host, praising God and singing:
>
> > 'Glory to God in the highest heaven,
> > and peace to all who enjoy his favor.' [64]

I have always been fascinated by this throng of winged presences and with their mysterious message. It is a message of peace. Wesley's hymn re-echoes the identical theme and names the newborn child "Prince of Peace." This title, in fact, comes to us from Isaiah (9:6) and is embedded in a passage which was interpreted by the early Christian community as a messianic prophecy foretelling the birth of Jesus.

Of the four gospel writers, Luke most clearly identifies the coming of Christ, and the new age which he inaugurates, with peace.[65] The evangelist draws heavily upon the texts of Isaiah and tends to image the Christ-event (as well as the birth of the Church, which he records in the Acts of the Apostles) as a fulfillment of Isaiah's promises, which are ripe with suggestions of peace. He, in fact, summarizes the life of Jesus in terms of peace.

> God sent his word to the people of Israel, and it was to them that the good news of peace was brought by Jesus Christ. . . .[66]*

The overtones of the term *peace*, when traced to its Hebrew roots, *shalom*, are rich. *Shalom* implies not simply the absence of conflict but also the blessings of God, a full and whole life, fertility of the land, and joy in community. *Shalom* is what is envisioned in the familiar blessings of Aaron that God is said to have spoken to Moses as recorded in Numbers.

> May Yahweh bless you and keep you.
> May Yahweh let his face shine on you and be gracious to you.
> May Yahweh uncover his face to you and bring you peace.[67]

Luke wants to say that all this—the fullness of life itself, God's saving reign of peace—is ushered in with the angelic proclamation in the countryside. And, the evangelist underscores this same point in the two famous songs he has placed in the gospel narrative, the Canticle of Zechariah and the Canticle of Simeon.

The first of these, which are generally thought to be early hymns from the Jewish-Christian community, is placed in the mouth of Zechariah, father of John the Baptist. While it portends the mission of his own son, this father's song focuses more directly on the quality of salvation inaugurated by the coming Messiah.

> His father Zechariah was filled with the Holy Spirit
> and spoke this prophecy:
> > 'Blessed be the Lord, the God of Israel,
> > for he has visited his people, he has come to their rescue
> > and he has raised up for us a power for salvation
> > in the House of his servant David,
> > even as he proclaimed,
> > by the mouth of his holy prophets from ancient times,
> > that he would save us from our enemies
> > and from the hands of all who hate us.
> > Thus he shows mercy to our ancestors,
> > thus he remembers his holy covenant,
> > the oath he swore

to our father Abraham
that he would grant us, free from fear,
to be delivered from the hands of our enemies,
to serve him in holiness and virtue
in his presence, all our days.
And you, little child,
you shall be called Prophet of the Most High,
for you will go before the Lord
to prepare the way for him.
To give his people knowledge of salvation
through the forgiveness of their sins;
this by the tender mercy of our God
who from on high will bring the rising Sun to visit us,
to give light to those who live
in darkness and the shadow of death,
and to guide our feet
into the way of peace.' [68]

We will have heard this ancient hymn proclaimed in the liturgy sometime during the Advent and Christmas seasons. But its stanzas are more deeply embedded in Christian consciousness than this seasonal reminder would suggest. For generations of devout Christians have had this canticle, traditionally known as the Benedictus, sung into the fabric of their prayer through the church's liturgy of the hours. This ancient hymn, along with the Canticle of Simeon and the Magnificat, were incorporated into the cyclical rhythm of the church's daily prayer from earliest times. Its final phrase echoes the angels' countryside annunciation. We are alerted to the fact that the cosmic event that comes to us wrapped in the meager covering of swaddling clothes has to do with walking in the path of peace. It is a about a richness and fullness of life only dreamed of previously. Luke has another prophetic figure present the same message somewhat later in the narrative. At the age of several weeks, the child Jesus is presented in the temple of Jerusalem, according to custom, because he is a first-born male. As it is recorded by Luke, at the ritual event there is a devout man, Simeon, who takes the baby in his arms and cries out:

> 'Now, Master, you can let your servant go in peace,
> just as you promised;
> because my eyes have seen the salvation
> which you have prepared for all the nations to see,
> a light to enlighten the pagans
> and the glory of your people Israel.' [69]

Simeon's song, known to posterity as the Nunc Dimittis, contains Luke's recurrent refrain, "Go in peace." Not simply a ritualized dismissal, the phrase combines a religious emphasis on the presence of God's saving power and the return of well-being with the normal biblical wish for a safe journey. Peace. God's *shalom*. In Luke's Gospel, the good news is encapsulated in the announcement of the coming of the Prince of Peace.

Peace on Earth

One of the most common greetings found inside contemporary holiday greeting cards is "Peace on Earth." Often, the sentiment is reproduced because it is a convenient yet thoughtful greeting that can be sent to any number of correspondents of varying faith perspectives or no faith perspective at all. Who could argue with a wish for peace? Everyone, everywhere seems to have the same articulated desire. Peace is desirable. Its seeming opposites—war, violence, chaos, and conflict—are not conditions to which people normally aspire.

Peace has universal appeal. Yet in the Christian context it is specifically associated with the person of Jesus Christ. The promised reign of God, the *shalom* prophesied by Isaiah, begins to be fulfilled in his birth. It is also manifested in his life. It is the living out of the promise of peace that must be our prayer and our struggle in the days following the Feast of the Nativity and throughout the year.

What is the peace of Christ? It is *shalom*–the fullness of life, the fertility of the land, the blessings of God, the joy of community. Such are the Hebrew roots of this notion. But how does one live this? In our contemporary violence-wracked world, the cry for peace is poignant and continual. But of what does God's peace consist?

Like the repentance we have been called to earlier in the season, peace has both outer and inner aspects. It is concerned with actions as well as dispositions of heart. The latter, outer, aspect of peace is the one we most obviously think of when we open our Christmas mail and find there cards embossed with white doves bearing olive branches in their beaks and the familiar "Peace on Earth" printed in fine, lined script. Certainly as Christians we are about envisioning and supporting ways of resolving conflicts on the international, national, and interpersonal levels that do not involve the use of force. Virtually every major Christian denomination has published official statements on the issue of war and peace, strongly affirming that Christians have the obligation to find alternatives to the use of armed force, especially in the present age in which nuclear capabilities make the waging of war an activity that can irreparably harm the entire global family.[70]

Luke's assignment of the title Prince of Peace to Jesus has enlivened the imaginations and shaped the quality of discipleship of many Christians over the centuries.[71] During the early era of the church's persecutions, many followers of Christ refused not only to worship the deities of the Roman rulers of their lands, they refused military service. On many levels of society, the small sect that followed the man Jesus, identified his mission with that of nonviolent peacemaking and a refusal to take up the sword. Later Christian responses to the waging of war varied greatly. After Christianity became an accepted religion within the larger society and then gradually became the religion of western culture, political and religious sensibilities tended to merge. Out of this came the famous "just war" theory, first hammered out by Augustine of Hippo in the fifth century, then expanded by Thomas Aquinas in the thirteenth. The waging of legitimate conflicts, within certain strict perimeters and always only as a last resort, became part of Christian thinking on warfare. Official ecclessial support of the use of force was most marked during the medieval era in the launching of the Crusades against what Christendom considered the infidels. Enthusiasm for holy wars like the Crusades ebbed by the sixteenth century at the same time that Christendom found itself torn apart by the Reformation and the ensuing Wars of Religion that bloodied the fields and holy places of Europe during the sixteenth and seventeenth centuries. It was during this era of fratricidal violence that the identification of Jesus as Prince of Peace, as one who models a way of nonviolent response to conflict, came once again to the fore. Several offshoot branches of the reform movement that tore Christian unity end to end saw their discipleship defined by the Prince who brings peace. The Anabaptists on the continent and the Quakers in England are the chief examples of Christian groups that embraced what they saw as a life of resignation to God in obedience to and imitation of Jesus who died in order for new life to be born. Jesus was for them the man of peace. Their churches patterned their moral guidelines on his example, seeing in his surrender on the cross a mandate to endure persecution and to work nonviolently against the ways of the world, which were the ways of violent triumph over enemies.

With the anthems of the angelic hosts still ringing in our ears, it is incumbent upon us as followers of this child whose arrival is haloed by the promise of peace to reflect seriously on the outer dimensions of our call to be peacemakers. We would do well to remember that we are accompanied in this task not only by generations of our forefathers and foremothers, but by modern day prophets of a vital and vibrant peace. American Christians should claim Martin Luther King, Jr., as their brother not only in the struggle to confront racism in our society, but in the struggle to play out on the international and national stage the beatitude, "blessed are the pacemakers." King's vision of social change was deeply rooted in Isaiah's prophecies. The goal of all of his nonviolent resistance to social evil was not the victory of a particular ideology or the passage of a particular law. The goal of non-violence was for King the creation of a "beloved community," a world in which the sad divisions that separate us, the enmities and fears that diminish us and cause us to inflict harm, might be transformed. The beloved community was to be one in which our common needs and desires take precedence over our separate concerns. It was to be a community in which all persons might be seen and celebrated as beloved children of the same God. It was to be a community that fulfilled the ancient prophecy:

> They will hammer their swords into ploughshares
> and their spears into sickles.
> Nation will not lift sword against nation,
> no longer will they learn how to make war.[72]*

The outer dimensions of peacemaking are almost endless. We exercise our call to be blessed peacemakers, not only when we work to find alternatives to armed force, but when we act as reconcilers and mediators in our places of work, in our communities, in our schools, and in our homes. As peacemakers we are not invited to avoid conflict, for conflict is inherent in the processes of growth and change. What we are asked to do is to negotiate creative conflict, to find new and transforming ways of resolving conflict that bypass the win-lose model of resolution in favor of resolutions in which all parties are mutually benefited.

In the face of a war-torn and violent world that we see reflected for us on the evening news, it is sometimes bewildering to know where to begin in becoming a peacemaker. While there are many organizations to which we might well belong and whose vigorous opposition to all that threatens the peace of our world–hunger, poverty, racism, violent nationalism, prejudices of all types, political and economic systems that oppress and victimize–is welcome, still there is another kind of peace work we are called to do. That is the work of nurturing our imaginations for peace. Essential to our response to the call is our sensitization to the creative dimensions of the peacemaker's task: a quickening of conscience and honing of imagination.

We are surrounded by vivid images of violence in our culture. But, for the most part, our images of peace are not equally compelling. We tend to see simply the absence of conflict when we dream of peace. Our positive images at best play themselves out as quiet domestic images: children unhindered at play near green-lawned, well-secured homes–a sort of practical-pig-who-built-the-brick-house-to-thwart-the-big-bad-wolf kind of imaging. Part of the peacemakers task, I believe, is to dare to imagine more richly and daringly than that. We need to truly image the fullness of the biblical *shalom.*

One of my favorite twentieth century artists who has made the fullness of peace more concrete for me is Fritz Eichenberg. Eichenberg is known for his woodcuts that decorated the pages of *The Catholic Worker* newspaper during the middle of this century. He quite literally depicted the prophecies of Isaiah, as well as other images from the tradition, in contemporary idiom. When I find myself lost for words, unanchored in my identity as peacemaker, I turn to Eichenberg for sustenance. His woodcuts allow my heart and mind to wrap around the fullness of *shalom.* A typical woodcut is his version of Isaiah 11:6-8. The black and white contrasts of the piece are striking. Clustered in front of a dark spreading tree, which itself is starkly outlined by the brightness of a gathering sunrise, are the beasts of the prophet's vision. Lion, ox, bear, goat, leopard, lamb, and wolf are cradled in pairs. In their midst a small boy child plays, a rabbit in his arms and a snake curled at his feet. Eichenberg's firm hand has captured the latent power and ferocity of the wild animals so that they seem not so much domesticated or de-fanged as they seem harnessed, their powerful energy gathered to bring their vitality to the gentler creatures.

I like too, the artist's "Peace on Earth" done in 1954. As one views it, the sad irony of our contemporary practices of "keeping the peace" leap into consciousness. An oversized wooden cross bearing the angel's greeting from the second chapter of Luke divides the picture into two parts. Under each of the cross' arms is a firmly etched figure facing inward. On the right, under a bright star, is a female angel whose human shape is clearly revealed by her softly draped gown; olive branches crown her head, and a white dove is held nestled against her breast. Across from her is a male soldier fully suited in the garb of modern combat: gas mask, helmet, heavy boots, gloves, and protective coverings obscure his natural frame. He cradles a cone-shaped metal bomb in his arms. The intrinsic violence of this heavily armed "peace keeper" contrasts dramatically with the unguarded vulnerability of the angel on the right. It is she to whom we would instinctively look when seeking for an image to express the biblical *shalom*.

Inner Peace

In the Roman communion January 1 is celebrated as a feast of peace. Within the cycle of readings that are heard during the twelve days after the Nativity are the readings from Numbers that contain the plaintive blessing of Aaron as well as Luke's annunciation to the shepherds. The tail end of the passage reads as follows:

> Now when the angels had gone from them into heaven, the shepherds said to one another, 'Let us go to Bethlehem and see

this thing that has happened which the Lord has made known to us.' So they hurried away and found Mary and Joseph, and the baby lying in a manger. When they saw the child they repeated what they had been told about him, and everyone who heard it was astonished at what the shepherds had to say. As for Mary, she treasured all these things and pondered them in her heart. And the shepherds went back glorifying and praising God for all they had heard and seen; it was exactly as they had been told.[73]

When informed of the numinous import of this birth, everyone who heard was astonished. Mary, especially, took heed and "treasured all these things and pondered them in her heart." For much of the church's history, the peace that Christ brings has been conceived of primarily as something that has to do with the heart. Peace is an inner disposition, an attitude of being, a quality of interiority which may also manifest itself outwardly. For centuries, when Christian contemplatives spoke of peace they referred to a sort of inner calm or detachment. *Apatheia* was the technical word for it. During the years when early Christian monastic spirituality was being formed, Greek philosophical notions of the life of virtue were incorporated into the tradition. Thus, the spiritual life became defined as a gradual overcoming of the passions. The spiritual warfare carried out within the heart of the hermit or monastic was warfare with the passions. To triumph over the passions was to be victorious with Christ over the powers of "world." Inordinate attachment and grasping covetousness were to give way to an inner freedom which the tradition loosely defined as "detachment." While the cultivation of such a spiritual state is in actuality a good deal more subtle than presented here, what happened is that biblical peace, especially the peace of Christ that passes all understanding, has been interpreted in our past to refer to such an interior spiritual attitude. Thus, to be a person of peace is to be someone who rises loftily above the anxieties of everyday life or remains unruffled in the face of difficulties or pain. A perfect example of this interpretation is found in a seventeenth century devotional classic (which I am otherwise very fond of), Brother Lawrence's *The Practice of the Presence of God*. In it, Brother Lawrence, who is a humble domestic member of a religious order and admired by many for his self-evident holiness, is described in the following manner:

> That as for the miseries and sins he heard of daily in the world, he was so far from wondering at them that, on the contrary, he was surprised that there were not more, considering the malice sinners were capable of; that, for his part, he prayed for them; but knowing that God could remedy the mischiefs they did when He pleased, he gave himself no further trouble.
>
> That to arrive at such resignation as God requires, we should watch attentively over all the passions which mingle as well in spiritual things as in those of a grosser nature; that God would give light concerning those passions to those who truly desire to serve Him.[74]

I am not sure, in the face of today's political and ecological realities, that such a vision of inner peace as Brother Lawrence espoused will allow us to act fully as Christians in the contemporary world. Peace, as a quality of heart, must more clearly reflect the richness of biblical *shalom*. It must have more to do with holding together in creative tension the terrible paradoxes of our lives. Fritz Eichenberg has several renderings of the Nativity which, I think, put into focus the quality of heart required for us as peacemakers in the present age. One of them, dated Christmas 1952, when America was involved in the Korean War, shows a naked, haloed infant with a distinctively Oriental slant to his closed eyes, resting in a bed of hay, adored by a donkey and a cow whose comforting looking bodies form a fleshy wedge within which the child is sheltered. A discarded soldier's helmet peeks out from the wisps of hay. The side wall of the stable is open, revealing a distant landscape in which a radiant star shines down upon a gutted countryside enveloped in flames. The woodcut juxtaposes two sights we are unaccustomed to seeing together: the baby in the manger and the ravages of war.

If we are to be truly peacemakers, I think we must move beyond the notion of peace as the absence of conflict, or in the case of inner peace, as detachment or lack of passion. Peace has to do with the fullness of things, with lion and lamb lying down together, not a world without lions. If we are to have hearts capable of the peace of Christ, which does indeed pass all understanding, we must have hearts capable of embracing the joy and the sorrow, the sacredness and the sin of the world. We must have hearts like Christ, in which all the terrible and disparate truths of human existence are held together in a searing, and ultimately, creative crucible. To have a heart of peace means knowing that we are not strangers to anything human, that we have within our selves the seeds of malice, violence, and death. Yet we also carry the seeds of joy, healing, and life. Those latter seeds will sprout when we have allowed our hearts to become places of ripening, places where can be realized a love so vast and courageous it transforms death into life.

In the Canticle of Zechariah, just before the ending stanza where Jesus is spoken of as one who leads our paths into the ways of peace, we find this:

> You shall be called. . . . to give his people knowledge of
> salvation through the forgiveness of their sins. . . .[75]

One of the greatest mysteries of our faith, a mystery foretold by Zechariah before Jesus' birth and enacted years later on the cross and announced in the post-Resurrection appearances, is the mystery of forgiveness. To forgive each other, to forgive ourselves, to forgive our enemies: this we are called to do. But the depth and width of the transformative power of forgiveness we rarely imagine. Forgiveness does not consist of merely saying we are sorry or allowing another to say it. Nor does it consist of sweeping away injustice or outrage as though it were all right. Rather, forgiveness is the capacity to transform a situation of pain or injustice into a situation that can generate new possibilities through unleashing all parties from the bondage in which they find themselves. Forgiveness involves rearranging the equations of our lives so that we suddenly discover a way out of impasse. To forgive means that we must be able to see each other anew, to entertain fresh beginnings, to nurture creative movement and new life. It means that we must be willing to peer into each other's hearts and discern there the seeds of goodness and healing. We must be capable of seeing ourselves in the other and the other in ourselves. No longer subject or object, ally or enemy, friend or stranger, one of us or one of them, saved or lost, chosen or cast out, we are not separate from or other than our seeming enemies, or the dark sides of ourselves.

The infant in the manger at Bethlehem comes with a message of peace, an announcement that all sad divisions, all the irreconcilable pieces of our public and private lives will be brought together in the celebration of *shalom*—God's blessing, God's peace. This will not, I think, occur when all conflict has ceased. For creative conflict is a necessary component of growth. Rather, peace will reign when our forgiveness of self and others is wide and deep enough to create new possibilities and, without the use of violence, to transform our seeming impasses into new freedoms and joy.

Walking in the Path of Peace

Whenever I can reach deep enough down through the ossified layers of my own inability to forgive and to genuinely become a peacemaker, I think of an incident which occurred to me a few years ago in Seattle where I was staying for several weeks while teaching a summer course.

The incident speaks to me of the Prince of Peace and of the kingdom he came to inaugurate.

Before coming to the state of Washington I had the opportunity to attend a workshop, sponsored by Pax Christi, the international Catholic peace movement, on nonviolent response to personal assault. The theory behind the workshop was that the principles of non-violent resistance, as elaborated by Martin Luther King, Jr., and others, could well be put into practice in the personal arena. As part of the weekend we watched a video in which several women were interviewed about their experiences of being personally assaulted and how they had applied the techniques of non-violence effectively to transform the situation from one of violent conflict to one of disarmament. Several ideas from the video on peacemaking, which I had to admit was more difficult to envision in this personal way than as public policy, stuck with me. First, assailants expect victims to respond as victimized. They expect fear or flight, and when they get it they play out their role as aggressor. Second, it is possible to look at someone else not as an enemy, but as another self. Third, doing so is disarming. So are any number of other unexpected responses that refuse to conform to the victim/victimizer scenario. Fourth, in an assault, you have as good a chance of surviving by using nonviolent means as you do using violent ones violent. In other words, there's never any guarantee (especially if a person is under the influence of a chemical substance, in which case very little works). Fifth, with the non-violent alternative you have the possibility of turning the situation around in a new way. A disarmed confrontation not only protects the potential victim, it often transforms the situation for the aggressor as well.

There were a number of extraordinary stories in the video such as the one in which a woman awakened in the night to find an armed man in her bedroom. She had the presence of mind to remain calm and confounded the intruder by asking him the time. He was so completely nonplused that he went into the kitchen to find a clock. They had a chat about time pieces and, completely disarmed, he allowed himself to be let out the back door. Not totally convinced, but impressed by the earnestness of these women's vision of dealing with violent confrontation, I carried these ideas away from the workshop.

Half a year later I found myself in downtown Seattle. I had finished teaching in the morning and had been told that I should not miss an excellent film playing in a nearby neighborhood. It was a beautiful summer afternoon and I was on foot. Deciding that I would catch the first show at around five, I set out to explore a bit of the city I had not seen before. It was so lovely, I thought, I will just take my books for tomorrow, find a sidewalk cafe somewhere after I locate the theater, and sit and read until five o'clock. My walk took me farther than I had anticipated and into a part of the city that made me a bit uneasy, being alone and on foot. But I cheered myself by staying on main streets and looking purposeful and invulnerable (like all the self-defense literature had always told me). I finally found the theater and began to look for a cafe. There were very few businesses in that area, and I found myself straying farther and farther from the main street, looking for someplace to read and get an iced tea. Finally I located a small snack shop where I could purchase an iced expresso or iced cafe au lait (you cannot just buy an iced tea in Seattle anymore). There was really no place to sit indoors, and the day was so sunny I decided to find a place outside. At the side of the building, around a corner and out of sight from the street, was a flight of public steps and a bench which looked like a likely stopping place. The neighborhood was a little too deserted and desolate feeling to make me very comfortable, and it did cross my mind that I probably should not have just put my purse next to me on the ground, but I did, dismissing my big-city paranoia offhand. I proceeded to get lost in my book.

About an hour later I was wrenched from my studious reverie by the sudden feeling that someone had come up quickly behind me and was moving toward my purse. Instinctively, I reached down and grabbed my bag. In the instant that I did so, the stranger came around my right side and planted himself directly in front of me. I was at the bottom of the steps and he was standing before me on the lowest step, so I basically had a glimpse of his shoes and knees, which gave me enough information to know that this was a man who had been on the street for some time. The time that elapsed between my moving my gaze from his knees to his face must have been only a few seconds, but they were the longest seconds I have ever experienced, and I learned much about him as they raced by. First, I was able to make a judgment about this man in terms of his strength and intent. He was about thirty to forty years of age, definitely down-and-out, but full of native agility and physical strength. He was (I later learned) half-Italian and half-Native American. His front teeth were missing. A string of tattoos curved up his arms. His hair was unkempt, as were his clothes. He was under the influence of some sort of substance.

In those same few seconds I had an astonishingly clearheaded conversation with myself. I knew that I was very frightened and I knew that I had two choices. One, I could act as frightened as I felt, perhaps draw back or lash out. Two, I could choose to see this man with eyes of love. (Those were the words that went through my mind.) A possible third choice, running, was not open to me because I was wedged in between the wall and the bottom of the steps and my visitor was in my line of escape. Somehow I summoned the presence to reach down into the depths of my heart and call up a reserve of love the likes of which I had never felt before. And when I finally looked into this man's eyes, I truly felt him to *be* myself. Our gazes met. For a brief moment I panicked. Whatever substance he was on blurred his eyesight and kept his gaze from meeting mine. Then, miraculously, he came into focus. He looked, then looked again, and his face softened, and he sat down right in front of me with his knees touching mine. "You're so pretty," he breathed, looking at me wonderingly, "and you're so *peaceful!*"

Then began one of the most remarkable two-hour segments of my life. The man asked my name. I told him. In fact, I told him five or six times during our talk because he kept lapsing in and out of clear consciousness, and my name kept getting lost in the process. He began to tell me about himself. His name was Sky Starhawk. He was half-Italian, half-Native American, and had been on a three-week drunk. His life had bottomed out. He told me about the woman he loved–a red-haired Scot who had sobered up and gone clean when she learned they were going to have a child. "I mean, she eats salad and yogurt now, like some sort of nun," Sky shook his head as he told me. She had gone home to Scotland before the birth, so he had never seen his child. During our conversation, Sky would quixotically move into a variety of moods. He would suddenly become violent, swearing about the f___ing trash on the streets, the Hell's Angels gang that was after him, the people he hated. And he would begin to get physically violent, swinging his arms around, punching into the air. Then he would become fascinated with me. He had a boat, or somebody he knew had a boat, and he really wanted me to come down and see it. At these moments I would begin to panic, fear rising up out of me and screaming at me to flee or fight. But something, some source of love, of centeredness, kept me with him. I was, I realized, more present to him than I had been to anyone in my life. There was a powerful field of the most gentle love that surrounded us. I watched in wonder as it kept drawing him deeper and deeper into the goodness of himself. He would look at me after one of his violent rampages and then seem reminded of some buried truth. He finally confessed that he could not go on this way much longer, that something in his life had to change. A friend had told him there was a place to go where you could make it by living one day at a time. But he was not sure he could do that. I told him I thought he could, that the very question he was raising about his life was evidence that he could, with help, turn it around. Then he showed me how to roll a cigarette. I thanked him for showing me but said I did not smoke. "Or do a lot of other things, I bet," Sky said. "You don't know how lucky you are," he breathed, blowing out the pain of his life with the smoke. But I did know how lucky I was, because he was no longer separate from me, I knew that his life was my life if it had not taken one or two different random turns.

We sat there, knee to knee for over two hours. I knew he did not want to let me go. But I told him I had to leave, and no, it would not be appropriate for him to come. Finally we stood up and he agreed to relinquish me. But before he did he took my hands and turned them palm up and kissed them tenderly. And then I left and walked, more briskly than I had ever walked, back to the movie theater and rushed inside. Needless to say, my nerves were taut and strained, which cast a rather surreal quality over my viewing the film. But I did not want to walk alone all the way back to the university just yet.

After seeing the Canadian film, which was a modern-day interpretation of the Christ story, I made my way back to my room and sought out several of my colleagues to help me deal with my day. As I was telling them about the incident, calling up my feelings about it, I knew they were resonating with my fear and wonder at what had happened. But there was something else that I felt that I could not give words to at that moment, something else that I knew but could not name.

It was not until much later that I was able to articulate what had happened to me, and to Sky, on that Seattle sidewalk on a weekday summer afternoon. We had been on holy ground. I had encountered the heart of another person in a way that was unimaginable to me before. We had been in the presence of a love that transformed us both and dissolved the glaring distance between our very different lives. I think I have never been as close to another person, at least for those few moments when Sky unwittingly lifted the heavy trappings that obscured his heart and let me, and himself, see the bare and beautiful personhood that was still aching there. Back in my room I sat at my desk with my head in my arms and prayed. And then I took off my shoes, as I should have in Sky's presence. For I had been on holy ground. And it was on fire. And it burned away all my neat theological categories and my comfortable cultural explanations in the heat of its flame.

If I could stand there again, I would know the peace of Christ that passes all understanding. I would be able to live God's *shalom*. At best perhaps, what I can do is to pray that my life and my perceptions, through struggle and fidelity, inch little by little toward that goal as the years unfold. But just for an instant I was privileged to walk firmly in the middle of the path of peace that the tiny babe of Bethlehem came to bring to us so long ago.

Light

I THINK BACK TO A DAY in the late 1980's when I first truly experienced the coming of the dawn. It astonishes me to think that a person can reach adulthood in our modern, industrialized society and never have viscerally experienced the transformative effects of the sun's first morning light. But, not growing up in a family that camped and not living in a rural area, my only experience was of an urban environment in which I could easily transform night into day with the flip of an electric switch. And the nighttime of my childhood was never genuinely dark, for the artificial glow of round-the-clock lighting hovers over any American metropolitan area like an out-of-sorts aura.

I was vacationing with in-laws in Breckenridge, Colorado, and had planned, mid-vacation, to drive over to Colorado Springs to give a quick paper at an academic conference and be back late the same day. To arrive in time for the first session, I needed to leave Breckenridge well before daylight, about four-thirty in the morning. Looking at the road map and trying to calculate the most direct route between the two cities was a bit tricky. There was no as-the-crow-flies route, for between them lay the great mass of the Rocky Mountains. Breckenridge was perched high on the mountain top, while Colorado Springs was nestled in the foothills more than three thousand feet lower in elevation. The most obvious itinerary would have been to take the highway east down the mountain to Denver, then cut south and west round the range to Colorado Springs. It would be broad interstates much of the way. But I did not really want to risk rush hour traffic skirting Denver and was loath to leave the romantic seclusion of the high mountains to pass through the noise and congestion of urban America. There was another way, the map informed me, although it was on back roads and, therefore, probably not as fast a route. I could climb over the mountains south of Breckenridge onto the high plains, cutting diagonally southeast through range land until I dipped down out of the hills into the valley where I would eventually come to Colorado Springs. There were no cities to pass through, only a very occasional remnant of a mining town or a national parks restroom stop.

The thought of the back route trip both intrigued and worried me. After all, it would be pitch black when I left, and I would be traveling over winding narrow roads that skirted sheer cliffs. And it was very cold, although the roads were crystal clear and no inclement weather was forecast. But I had a sturdy, well-serviced car; and once I got over the mountain pass, which would take about an hour and a half, I would be moving into lower, warmer elevations and would be headed into the rising sun. I decided to go the back route.

Early on the appointed morning I slipped on my clothes for the conference, grabbed a cup of hot tea and a bagel, and headed out the door without disturbing any of my soundly sleeping family. It was dark, darker than I'd ever seen. The faint light streaming from the condominium entryway allowed me to locate my keys and find my car door lock, but once I had driven a quarter mile out the back road of town, I was enveloped in inky blackness. The two insignificant tunnels of light fanning out from my car headlights were swallowed up by the blackness a few brief feet in front of me. I drove very slowly. Peering ahead, I saw a thin snake of road wind up the mountainside and disappear in a velvet curtain of night. Well, here goes, I thought, creeping up the mountain, my frozen breath hanging in small clouds around me inside the car. I began my ascent. Hairpin turn after hairpin turn, I navigated the thin lip of the road's edge cautiously. At each turn my headlights pierced a few feet of darkness, giving me a momentary glimpse of the dizzying cliffs that rose across the road to my left and the seemingly bottomless chasms that gaped open near my wheels on the right. Night was so dense you could cut it with a knife. I was vigilantly alert. While my mind continued to assure me that there was no danger on these dry roads as long as I went slowly and stayed aware, my heart kept faltering. This was pretty nerve-wracking. Maybe I should call the whole thing off. But not only was there a seminar full of people down in the valley who would be assembling and waiting for me to arrive, there also seemed to be no easy way to turn around on the narrow mountain road. And going back down would not be any easier than going farther up. Eventually, I knew, I would reach the crest and a wider road that passed through less treacherous terrain. I surrendered to the experience and kept inching along.

So this is night, I heard myself saying to myself, the child familiar with the glow of bedroom night-lights and the companionship of streetlights that peer in through living room windows. The mountain dark was neither ominous nor potentially danger filled, as are the unlit alley ways of a city. It was wonderfully ripe with a sense of vital presence. And it was vast and star-filled.

Finally I reached the crest. By that time the inky blackness had begun to pale to charcoal gray. My field of vision was thus somewhat enlarged, and I could begin to make out features of the terrain, the trees and rocks, the changing contours of the land. The road leading down off the crest was less winding, and soon it leveled out, and I found myself at the edge of the high mountain plains commanding a view that must have stretched for fifty miles. The first rays of the sun began to show on the horizon. I was alone, on the top of the world. Not another soul was evident. The light from the rising sun grew brighter as I began my descent. Gray turned to pale dawn yellows, then to vivid red-browns and gold. The sky stretched wide from horizon to horizon, the broad sweep of the plains made an earthen vessel into which the sun poured its increasingly brilliant light.

The coming of the light. With its dawning came vision, clarity, and warmth. For the next hour I traversed that high mountain range land, until the road crossed over the next plateau and began its hilly descent toward the distant valley. It was an hour spent bathed in the wonder of light. How little, until then, had I known the life-giving power of the sun's light. How unspeakably glorious it was. And how independent of us. We may simulate its brightness as we illuminate our twenty-four-hour-a-day lives, we may harness its energies for our own purposes in our own time, but the great globe of the sun does not finally rise or set at our convenience, nor does it pour forth its healing growth-giving energy simply for us. There on that high crest of the world the sun blazed in unimaginable beauty, bathing the earth in a riot of daytime colors for no one at all. I was a stray, happenstance recipient of a sight that memory and words cannot adequately convey. I had known light.

The Coming of the Light

Since earliest times the Christian community has utilized light as a primary symbol to convey the meaning of the Christ-event. The power of the symbol was not lost on most generations of believers who lived closer than we do to the truth that we are all ultimately dependent upon the light of the sun for warmth, vision, and life itself. The symbol was not new with the Christian faith, but has its direct antecedent in the prophesies of Isaiah. It is the Hebrew prophet's ringing words that we commonly find proclaimed as the first reading on the Feast Day of Epiphany.

> Arise, shine out, for your light has come,
> the glory of Yahweh is rising on you,
> though night still covers the earth
> and darkness the peoples.

Above you Yahweh now rises
and above you his glory appears.
The nations come to your light
and kings to your dawning brightness.

Lift up your eyes and look round:
all are assembling and coming towards you,
your sons from far away
and your daughters being tenderly carried.

At this sight you will grow radiant,
your heart throbbing and full;
since the riches of the sea will flow to you,
the wealth of the nations come to you;

Camels in throngs will cover you,
and dromedaries of Midian and Ephah;
everyone in Sheba will come,
bringing gold and incense
and singing the praise of Yahweh.[77]

In early Christian circles this passage was claimed as a prophecy foretelling the coming of Christ. It is light which is the dominant image here, light as the dawning of a new day, light as the shining glory of Yahweh, light as the power that overcomes darkness, light as the sovereign majesty of God who brings fulfillment of promise and to whom all earthly rulers must bow. Christ becomes the divine light that bathes all created life in its healing rays.

Light imagery also permeated the writings of the fathers of the church. And the brilliant star that beckoned the shepherds and wise men to follow its lead was sometimes seen as a harbinger of the light that comes to overturn the principalities and powers of the world. Patristic literature is suffused with the language of cosmic tension: of the struggle between the prince of the world and the prince of peace, the struggle between the powers of dark and death and the powers of light and new life. One of my favorite passages comes from Ignatius of

Antioch, a second century Syrian bishop who was condemned to die for his faith by being thrown to beasts in the amphitheaters of Rome. His last journey took him to various Christian churches ringing the Mediterranean, including the one in Ephesus. In gratitude for their hospitality and to confirm his companions in their faith, he wrote of the world-reversing victory of Christ in imitation of whom he was about to die. His letter to the Ephesians records his vibrant faith. The imagery of light is woven through the text.

> And the virginity of Mary and her giving birth were hidden from the Prince of the world, as was also the death of the Lord. Three mysteries of a cry which were wrought in the stillness of God. How then was he manifested in the world? A star shone in heaven beyond all the stars, and its light was unspeakable, and its newness caused astonishment, and all the other stars, with the sun and moon, gathered in chorus round this star, and it far exceeded them all in its light; and there was perplexity whence came this new thing, so unlike them. By this all magic was dissolved and every bond of wickedness vanished away, ignorance was removed, and the old kingdom was destroyed, for God was manifest as man for the "newness" of eternal life, and that which had been prepared by God received its beginning. Hence all things were disturbed, because the abolition of death was being planned.[78]

Creation Transfigured

That something of momentous import occurred when God took human flesh is affirmed in this passage from Ignatius, something so remarkable that the face of the cosmos was forever changed. This sense of radical change, of the transfiguration of the creation itself, is most keenly expressed in the spirituality of Eastern Orthodox Christianity. It is in the East that Epiphany (or as it is known there, Theophany–divine manifestation), as a feast on the church's calendar, has retained some of the centrality that it had in the early church. For in fact, until the fourth century, this feast, along with Easter and

Pentecost, were the three major Christian feasts. In those early centuries the Nativity and the Baptism of the Lord were celebrated together on Epiphany. Gradually, the Nativity became a separate feast. Epiphany became a time on the eastern calendar for celebrating the Lord's Baptism and for emphasizing the radical newness that Christ brings. The scriptural account of the baptism is depicted in Matthew's version as follows:

> As soon as Jesus was baptised he came up from the water, and suddenly the heavens opened and he saw the Spirit of God descending like a dove and coming down on him. And a voice spoke from heaven, 'This is my Son, the Beloved; my favour rests on him.' [79]

In Eastern Orthodox churches it is customary to display a special icon (a holy image) in the church sanctuary for each discreet feast day. Icons in that tradition are not like religious art in the Western world. They are not primarily teaching devices, nor are they products of aesthetic devotion. They are, rather, windows on the divine. They show forth the truths of the divine life. They are impressions of heavenly archetypes upon matter itself. The icon displayed for the Feast of Epiphany is the icon of the baptism of the Lord. Conveyed in the imagery of the baptismal icon is the idea that Christ comes to the waters not for cleansing but to reconsecrate creation. The water, in ancient association, represents both life and chaos. Thus, in some versions of the icon the waters of the Jordan contain a little person—the personification of the river itself that is associated with the evil of the world—who is being chased away. It is the triumph of new life and the reversal of the powers of death that is communicated here, just as it is in Ignatius of Antioch's letter to the Ephesians.

That creation itself is radically renewed by Christ's coming is evident in the writings of another patristic figure, Clement of Alexandria.

> Where he came from and who he was, he showed by what he taught and by the evidence of his life. He showed he was the herald, the reconciler, our Saviour, the Word, a spring of life and peace flooding over the whole face of the earth. Through him, to put it briefly, the universe has already become an ocean of blessings.[80]

Coming to grips with this profound intuition of cosmic renewal, so central to the Eastern Orthodox conception of Christianity, is part of what it means to live the season of the Coming. The Eastern world most clearly articulates it at the Feast of the Transfiguration (observed on August sixth), which recalls the appearance of Christ in all his glory during his earthly life. The Transfiguration is chronicled in the Gospels of Matthew, Mark, and Luke. In each of these accounts Jesus is seen by his disciples, transfigured in light, flanked by Hebrew prophets. Matthew recounts the event this way:

> Jesus took with him Peter and James and his brother John and led them up a high mountain where they could be alone. There in their presence he was transfigured: his face shone like the sun and his clothes became as white as the light. Suddenly Moses and Elijah appeared to them; they were talking with him. Then Peter spoke to Jesus 'Lord,' he said, 'it is wonderful for us to be here; if you wish, I will make three tents here, one for you, one for Moses and one for Elijah.' He was still speaking when suddenly a bright cloud covered them with shadow, and from the cloud there came a voice which said, 'This is my Son, the Beloved; he enjoys my favour. Listen to him.' When they heard this, the disciples fell on their faces, overcome with fear. But Jesus came up and touched them. 'Stand up,' he said, 'do not be afraid.' And when they raised their eyes they saw no one but only Jesus.[81]

The two feasts of the Transfiguration and Epiphany (Theophany) are linked in Orthodox sensibilities by the fact that these two feasts commemorate the only two times that the Divine Trinity itself was made manifest. At the time of Jesus' baptism in the Jordan, when the Holy Spirit descended and the heavenly voice announced the divine Sonship (Matthew 3:13-17; Mark 1:9-11; Luke 3:21-22; John 1:29-34), the first manifestation occurred. The second and final showing forth took place on the mountain top during the course of Jesus' ministry (Matthew 17:1-13; Mark 9:2-13; Luke 9:28-36). In this case, the Trinitarian presence is represented by first, the divine voice, which recapitulates the affirmation made at the time of the baptism that "This is my beloved Son"; second, by Jesus himself; and third, (depending on the gospel commentator) either the light of transfiguration or the overshadowing cloud representing the presence of the Spirit.

Both of these feasts, when viewed through the eyes of faith, cry out that in the Christ event the cosmos is renewed, and creation has become, to use Clement of Alexandria's poetic phrase, "an ocean of blessings." It is especially the latter feast, the Transfiguration, that is a feast of light. And it is light which Orthodoxy presents to us as the core of living the season. At the heart of the spirituality of Eastern Christianity is the notion that the divine light permeates the world. That branch of Christianity puts forward the doctrine of deification, the teaching that God became human in order that humans might participate in God. The human person, since the incarnation, is seen to be a new creation. The vocation of the individual person is thus to fully realize this newness to become transfigured light. To do this, one embarks on a discipline of prayer and asceticism so that the true nature of the person now conjoined with Christ—the divine light that permeates creation—might become visible. The doctrine of deification, while it has roots deep in past tradition, was systematically elaborated in the fourteenth century by the Byzantine monk, archbishop, and theologian, Gregory Palamas. Palamas asserted that, as a participant in the body of Christ, a Christian is penetrated with divine life or the "energy" of uncreated light. There is real communion between the Uncreated God and creatures and real deification.

> In his incomparable love for men, the Son of God . . . becomes one body with us making us a temple of the whole Godhead–for in the very Body of Christ the whole fullness of the Godhead dwells corporeally (Col. 3:9). How then would he not illuminate those who share worthily in the divine radiance of his Body within us, shining upon their soul as he once shone on the bodies of the apostles on Tabor? For as this Body, the source of the light of grace . . . shone exteriorly on those who came near it worthily, transmitting light to the soul through the eyes of sense. But today, since it is united to us and dwells within us, it illuminates the soul interiorly.[82]

The analogy of the sun's light is often used to describe this stunning vision of the transfigured creation. Just as the rays of the sun are not identical to the sun itself but participate in it, so the divine energies that permeate creation are not identical with the essence of divinity, yet they participate in it in a real way. Thus uncreated light in the form of energy illuminates the soul from within. The task is to come to *see* the light, to see the transfiguration of the cosmos that has taken place. Orthodox commentators on the Transfiguration often point out that the light that the apostles saw radiating from Jesus on the mountain was not simply present in Jesus himself, but in the eyes of those who beheld him. The Transfiguration is thus also a feast that celebrates *our* deification, *our* increasing capacity to behold the divine light irradiating all creation. Thus it is the vocation of all baptized Christians to become living icons, transparent windows through which the light of divine life pours. This is the ultimate search of human life, to become seers and bearers of that light. A Christmas sermon delivered by the nineteenth century Orthodox theologian, Metropolitan Philaret of Moscow, witnesses to this truth.

> From the moment the divinity existed in humanity, all the gifts of His divine power that belong to life and to piety were communicated to us and that is why our weakness will be filled with divine strength, our lies cleansed by divine truth, our darkness illuminated by divine light. . . . That is the glorious mystery and mysterious glory of this day! The heavenly servants of light saw the dawn of glory before we did, and at once they alerted us, crying out: "Glory to God in the highest of the heavens." Now it is no longer dawn but high noon of that glory: may our glory also dawn, may it in turn ascend to those who dwell in heaven.[83]

In response to this breathtaking vision of creation transfigured by light, the Orthodox world offers worship and praise. For all of us then, living the season consists in part of cultivating our capacity for renewed seeing. This we do by prayer, by song, by praise, by gratitude. In a word, through worship in its most ecstatic sense, a worship which transfigures us to fully become the light.

Following the Star

In the Western church, from the fourth century, the Feast of Epiphany gradually lost its baptismal character. It also was separated from the Feast of the Nativity. It became identified primarily as a feast that celebrated the manifestation of Christ to the Gentiles. Thus, it was the biblical stories of the magi and their following the star that have come to inform the symbolism of the liturgy in the Western world.

> After Jesus had been born at Bethlehem in Judaea during the reign of King Herod, some wise men came to Jerusalem from the east. 'Where is the infant King of the Jews?' they asked. 'We saw his star as it rose and have come to do him homage.' When King

Herod heard this he was perturbed, and so was the whole of Jerusalem. He called together all the chief priests and the scribes of the people, and enquired of them where the Christ was to be born. 'At Bethlehem in Judaea,' they told him, 'for this is what the prophet wrote:

> And you, Bethlehem, in the land of Judah,
> you are by no means least among the leaders of Judah,
> for out of you will come a leader
> who will shepherd my people Israel.'

Then Herod summoned the wise men to see him privately. He asked them the exact date on which the star had appeared, and sent them on to Bethlehem. 'Go and find out all about the child,' he said, 'and when you have found him, let me know, so that I too may go and do him homage.' Having listened to what the king had to say, they set out. And there in front of them was the star they had seen rising; it went forward and halted over the place where the child was. The sight of the star filled them with delight, and going in to the house they saw the child with his mother Mary, and falling on their knees they did him homage. Then, opening their treasures, they offered him gifts of gold and frankincense and myrrh. But they were warned in a dream not to go back to Herod, and returned to their own country by a different way.[84]

The loving legend of centuries of devotion has elaborated upon Matthew's narrative, and given personalities to the three magi (which means great or illustrious men), making them kings from the mysterious East. Bede the Venerable, eighth century historian, in retelling the legend of the magi depicted the first as Melchior, a bearded, white-haired old man bearing gold; the second as Caspar, a young, beardless, ruddy-hued fellow bringing incense; and the third as Baltasar, a heavily-bearded, black-complexioned man carrying myrrh. Throughout France, Belgium, and Middle Europe the dramatization of the story of the three magi was a customary feature of the Christmas celebration for centuries. Out of this tradition of popular piety comes some of our favorite seasonal music like the nineteenth century "We Three Kings."

> *We three kings of Orient are;*
> *bearing gifts we traverse afar,*
> *field and fountain, moor and mountain*
> *following yonder star.*

> *O star of wonder, star of light,*
> *star with royal beauty bright,*
> *westward leading, still proceeding*
> *guide us to thy perfect light.*

The pageantry and color of this royal oriental procession replete with its camels (recalling the imagery of Isaiah 60), its rich fabrics, and its opulent treasures is an integral part of Christmas time lore. As a moment of insight into the Christian revelation, the Feast of Epiphany speaks to the universality of God's gift of the Christ. The magi become representatives of the "Gentiles," the non-Jewish peoples of the earth. Thus God's special covenantal relationship established with the people of Israel, which, according to revelation, is fulfilled in Jesus, becomes available to all people. The Christ event is shown forth to all nations (*epiphany* means "manifestation" or "showing forth" in Greek).

Such is the salvific proclamation of the feast as observed in the West. But the devotion of generations has teased out further themes from the magi's story, the evidence of which we find encased in story, folk song and legends.

One such theme is that of gift giving. We see this theme played out, in commercial excess, everywhere in contemporary American culture. What began, in centuries past, as a custom of bringing gifts to the Christ child and later became a practice of exchanging gifts to express affection and respond to real need has now become in our culture a veritable orgy of conspicuous consumption. Yet we still tell stories about the true nature of giving gifts throughout the season. We have a recent and popular Christmastide song, "The Little Drummer Boy," that, in rather sentimental fashion, recalls for us the truth that it is not our material possessions that must be brought before God, but the naked gift of self. It is sung to the percussive rolling of a drum.

> *Come, they told me (pa rum pum pum pum)*
> *Our newborn king to see (pa rum pum pum pum)*
> *Our finest gifts we'll bring (pa rum pum pum pum)*
> *To lay before the king (pa rum pum pum pum, rum pum*
> *pum pum, rum pum pum pum)*
> *So to honor him (pa rum pum pum pum)*
> *When he comes.*

> *Baby Jesus (pa rum pum pum pum)*
> *I am a poor boy too (pa rum pum pum pum)*
> *I have no gift to bring (pa rum pum pum pum)*
> *To lay before a king (pa rum pum pum pum, rum pum*
> *pum pum, rum pum pum pum)*
> *Shall I play for you (pa rum pum pum pum) on my drum?*
> *On my drum?*

> *Mary nodded (pa rum pum pum pum)*
> *The ox and lamb kept time (pa rum pum pum pum)*
> *I played my drum for him (pa rum pum pum pum)*
> *I played my best for him (pa rum pum pum pum, rum*
> *pum pum pum, rum pum pum)*
> *Then he smiled at me (pa rum pum pum pum)*
> *Me and my drum.*

The carol focuses on what we truly have to give—not our wealth, position, or power, but rather our native talents and the generosity of our hearts that are willing to give what we are rather than what we have.

Any number of popular Yuletide tales carry the same message. Among them is the justly renowned *Gift of the Magi* by the American short story writer O. Henry. The story recalls the Christmas gift exchange of a young couple recently married who, because they are struggling to get by, have no extra money to buy each other Christmas presents. Secretly each of them plans to fete the other with a surprise. The young husband hopes to buy a set of elegant tortoise shell combs for his wife's beautiful long hair. She in turn wants so to purchase a fob chain for the gold watch which is his one treasure. Since neither has the money to buy these extravagant gifts, each plans to sacrifice something precious to procure the needed funds. The wife sells her beautiful long hair while the husband sells his watch. What they quickly discover is that their real gift to one another was the gift of love. By giving up what was most prized to them, they gave themselves.

The gifts of gold, frankincense, and myrrh which the kings offered so ceremoniously to the Christ child are at the heart of the season and hold importance beyond the Christmas cycle into the following year. They represent the gifts that we all bring to that same stable each year of our lives.

We have a tendency in American culture to conceive of gifts and gift-giving in two primary ways, neither of which captures the soul of the season. First, we think of gifts as objects, things, commodities to be exchanged. And, we tend to value gifts by their relative material value–if it costs more, it must be better. This is obviously a distortion of the truth so tenderly told in O. Henry's story: A genuine gift involves a giving of the very substance of who we are. It means giving away or giving up. It involves some sort of dying on our part. We all know the experience of receiving a gift from someone that is that kind of gift. A hand-crocheted item designed for us by a friend, a poem or a piece of music especially composed, a crayoned picture from a child that represents hours of labor, the priceless gift of time or attentive listening, a gesture of love that frees or heals, an act of kindness or compassion—all these, and many others, carry with them the gift of self, the only true gift.

Secondly, we tend to think of our talents and abilities, our gifts, as given to us to develop so that we might realize our own potential. In our generous, egalitarian way we want everyone to be free and given the opportunity to become the person they might become. What we miss, when we think in our uniquely American individualistic way, is the secret that lies at the heart of the gift giving of the three kings. It is the secret that lies at the heart of the Christian message. It is this: that our gifts are given to us for the life of the whole community. We are not separate lives becoming more and more actualized for our individual salvation or self-realization or creative unfolding. We are intertwined on levels so complex and deep that we are best described, as Saint Paul so aptly does, as one body, one integral organism with its life source stemming from the swaddled infant cradled in the manger in Bethlehem. Our particular gifts are given so that the entire body might be fully alive. While we may seemingly be fulfilled in the process of bringing our gifts to maturity, in the end it is clear that we have only that which we give away. We are givers of life for one another, not hoarders of our riches for ourselves. Like seed, our gifts only truly flower when they are sown in the fields of the community, tended and harvested and distributed for the nourishment of all.

Our mutual gift-giving takes place on many levels. We all share the work of being church, a community of mutual need and nourishment that enables each of us to feed and be fed. We worship together, serve on committees, sing in the choir, teach Sunday school, preside, preach, decorate the altar, serve as lay ministers, and on and on. We share our lives in story, in peer ministry, in support groups, Bible study, pastoral counseling, feeding the hungry, sheltering the homeless, visiting the sick, and more. We share the deepest desires of our hearts in prayer, in intercession, in spiritual direction and friendship, in mutual compassion, and other ways. At the end of our star-gazing journey we spill out the richness of our lives upon one another, upon the Christ. To follow the light is to find the source of light and become that light ourselves.

Seeking for the Deepest Meaning

Another persistent theme which the collective Christian imagination has culled from the gospel narratives involving the star is the theme of the call and the search. One of my favorites among Christmas carols is the Afro-American spiritual, "Rise Up, Shepherd." The initial melody bursts forth in the upper register like the clarion call of a horn.

> *There's a star in the East on Christmas morn!*
> > (Then the insistent pulsing reply comes)
> *Rise up shepherd and follow.*
> > (Again, the clarion proclamation)
> *It will lead to the place where the Saviour's born!*
> > (And the reply, more gently this time)
> *Rise up shepherd and follow.*
>
> *Leave your sheep and leave your lambs*
> *Rise up, shepherd and follow*
> *Leave your ewes and leave your rams*
> *Rise up shepherd and follow.*
>
> *Follow, follow, rise up shepherd and follow*
> *Follow the star of Bethlehem*
> *Rise up shepherd and follow.*
> *If you take good heed to the angel's words,*
> *Rise up shepherd and follow*
> *You'll forget your flocks*
> *You'll forget your herds*
> *Rise up shepherd and follow.*

The tune's stirring melody conjures up images of the bent and burdened slaves of America's cotton fields suddenly standing erect, alert to hear the call. The music's cadence and modulations, so distinctive of black spirituals, carry with them the liberated hope of a people oppressed. For this baby, whose star shone over the manger at Bethlehem, is the Jesus whom Christians of African-American descent have known as the one who suffers with human oppression and pain and who ultimately frees humans from such conditions.

His is a call that frees. But the call is only one part of the imagery of the star's season into which the Christian community has lived. The call is not an ending but a beginning. The birth of the baby invites us into a search. I think the simple truth that is being held out here is that at its richest the Christian life is not so much a life lived as though all the answers were given, but a life lived as though all our answers are only gateways into deeper levels of answering, which in turn lead us into mystery where all answers give way to bended knee and adoration and praise. This truth was once presented to me in a form that I have never forgotten. A novice master of a Trappist monastery I once visited offered this observation: To be a Christian does not mean knowing all the answers; to be a Christian means being willing to live in the part of the self where the question is born.

In other words, it means being a genuine seeker after God. Folk legends from a number of cultures have given us access to this idea through the medium of narrative. My favorite is the story of Babushka. This variant is of Russian origin, but similar tales are found in many eastern European folk traditions.

Babushka is a person who, like many of us, is oh-so-busy. A tidy housekeeper, always occupied with the myriad chores that seem to need doing, she is too busy one evening to find out about the commotion in the village. All her neighbors are out, gossiping about a bright star overhead and a nearing caravan of royalty. Babushka is soon startled to hear a knock at her door. Three richly dressed kings ask her if they can lodge overnight, since she has the finest house in the village. The foreigners stay and tell her they are following the bright star. Why doesn't she come too? They are bringing gifts to a prophesied newborn king. His star is leading them on their way. But Babushka doesn't feel as though she has a proper gift. And my, what a mess these visitors have made. She simply must stay and clean up. She will come the next day. So the kings leave without her. But when her cleaning work is done and after she has prepared a proper gift, Babushka feels the urgent need to catch up with the dignitaries. They are a full day's journey ahead of her, but she sets out. Everywhere she asks for the kings until she tracks them to the village of Bethlehem, where she is told they have come and gone. And so has the baby. The child is the Savior of the world, and Babushka has missed him! So she continues her search year after year, for time means nothing in the search for things that are real. Legend relates that she can still be seen in villages at Christmas time, looking for the Christ child. "Is he here? Is he here?"

Babushka is all of us, busy with our myopic pursuits, too preoccupied with short-range concerns to respond when the call to truly encounter God comes. Yet there is in us the persistent intuition that we have indeed been called and that we must follow. So, too late and unprepared, we rush off on the search. And seek we do, led by the beckoning light of the star which illuminates a path in our darkness. We are Babushka, and we are seeking for the deepest meaning of our lives.

Keeping the Vigil

EACH YEAR the season of the Coming ends. Yet our seeking never does. We know that next year the season will entice us once again into its unique play of image, word, and song that will take us to the gates of inexpressible mystery. It is good that the season comes around again each year, for we never will exhaust its richness at any given moment. Each time we encounter and pray with the season we move deeper and deeper into the vigil itself. The stories of our lives gradually become woven into the fabric of the cosmic story being told. We penetrate more profoundly the layers of the Mystery the church proclaims.

We locate the sacred in a season. During Advent we continue to learn what it is to believe the promises, prepare and repent, rejoice, wonder, and dream. On the Nativity we learn anew to welcome silence, our poverty, and the momentous fact that God is with us and asks us to bear Christ to the world. During the Twelve Days we learn once again that the Coming is lived out in the midst of darkness, both personal and communal, and that we are called to walk the paths of peace, aware of the reality of transfigured light in our midst, yet searching ardently to live in the light, sharing our gifts with one another, bringing each other into the fullness promised so long ago.

The liturgical year opens the present to both the past and the future, widening our vision to glimpse the timelessness of God's own time. Through it we enter into the vigil being kept in the season before seasons. We continue to wait for the fullness. We watch for the completion of the promise. We keep vigil for the Coming of the unimaginable fruition of the seed growing from the beginning in the heart of God.

Omaha, Nebraska
Advent, 1991

Notes

WAITING

1. "The Call" from "The Temple, Sacred Poems and Private Ejaculations" in *George Herbert: The Country Parson, The Temple*, ed. John N. Wall, Jr. (New York: Paulist Press, 1981), p. 281.

Promise

2. On this mountain, Yahweh Sabaoth will prepare . . . (Isaiah 25:6).
3. He will destroy death forever (Isaiah 25:8).
4. Then the eyes of the blind shall be opened . . . (Isaiah 35:5-6).
5. Let the desert and the dry lands be glad . . . (Isaiah 35:1-2).
6. The wolf will live with the lamb . . . (Isaiah 11:6-9).
7. They will hammer their swords into ploughshares . . . (Isaiah 2:4).
8. The Lord himself, therefore, will give you a sign . . . (Isaiah 7:14).
9. For there is a child born for us . . . (Isaiah 9:5-7).
10. The spirit of the Lord Yahweh has been given to me . . . (Isaiah 61:1-3).
11. The reader interested in pursuing the rich history of the infancy narratives with the guidance of sound biblical scholarship is referred to Raymond E. Brown's *An Adult Christ at Christmas* (Collegeville, Minnesota: Liturgical Press, 1978) or to his much longer *The Birth of the Messiah* (Garden City, NY: Doubleday, 1977).
12. I am going to create a new heavens and a new earth . . . (Isaiah 65:17, 19-20, 66:10).

Preparation

13. About times and dates . . . (1 Thessalonians 5:1-3, 6).
14. A voice cries in the wilderness . . . (Luke 3:4-6).
15. He said, therefore, to the crowds . . . (Luke 3:7-9, 16-17).
16. *The Sermons of St. Francis de Sales for Advent and Christmas*, trans. by Nuns of the Visitation, ed. Fr. Lewis S. Fiorelli, O.S.F.S., Vol. IV of *The Sermons of St. Francis de Sales* (Rockford, Illinois: Tan Book and Publishers, 1987), pp. 45-46.
17. . . . he shall judge the poor with justice . . . (Isaiah 11:4-5).
18. When all the people asked him . . . (Luke 3:10-14).
19. Go back and tell John what you have seen and heard . . . (Luke 7:22-23).

Rejoice

20. Always be joyful, then, in the Lord . . . (Philippians 4:4-7).
21. My soul proclaims the greatness of the Lord . . . (Luke 1:46-55).
22. An accessible and beautifully illustrated introduction to Mary in the Christian tradition is Lawrence Cunningham, *Mother of God* (San Francisco: Harper and Row, 1982).
23. "Selected Praises of Mary from the Agathestos Hymn" (Greek, sixth century) found in Cunningham, *Mother of God*, p. 123.
24. This sonnet is taken from a seven-sonnet sequence of Donne's known as "La Corona" (The Crown), cf. *The Complete Poetry of John Donne*, ed. John T. Shawcross (New York: Doubleday Anchor Books, 1967), pp. 334-335. I have modernized the spelling.
25. Pierre Teilhard de Chardin, *Hymn of the Universe*, trans. Gerald Vann O.P. (New York: Harper and Row, 1969), pp. 69-70.
26. For a scholarly appraisal of the theme of liberation in the infancy narratives see Richard A. Horsley, *The Liberation of Christmas: The Infancy Narratives in Social Context* (New York: Crossroad Books, 1989).
27. *The Gospel in Art by the Peasants of Solentiname*, ed. Philip and Sally Scharper (Maryknoll, New York: Orbis Books, 1984), p. 8.

Wonder

28. "The Oxen" in *The Complete Poems of Thomas Hardy* (New York: Macmillan, 1978), p. 468.
29. . . . an angel of the Lord appeared to him in a dream . . . (Matthew 1:20-22).
30. . . . the angel of the Lord appeared to Joseph in a dream . . . (Matthew 2:19-21).
31. On the formative power of images in the tradition see Margaret R. Miles, *Image as Insight: Visual Understanding in Western Christianity and Secular Culture* (Boston: Beacon Press, 1985).
32. Readers interested in the contemporary dialogue between religion and science that is shaping interest in a creation-centered theology are referred to Thomas Berry and Thomas Clark, *Befriending the Earth: A Theology of Reconciliation Between Humans and the Earth* (Mystic, Connecticut: Twenty-Third Publications, 1991).
33. . . . at the hour of the incense, the whole congregation was outside praying . . . (Luke 1:10-12).
34. In the sixth month the angel Gabriel was sent . . . (Luke 1:26-30).
35. In the countryside close by there were shepherds . . . (Luke 2:8-9).

The Coming

36. *The Prayers of Catherine of Siena*, ed. Suzanne Noffke, O.P. (New York: Paulist Press, 1983), 148.

Silence

37. *Johannes Tauler: Sermons*, trans. Maria Shrady (Mahwah, New Jersey: Paulist Press, 1985), p. 35.
38. In the beginning was the Word . . . (John 1:1-3).
39. *Ibid.*, p. 36.
40. Angelus Silesius, *The Cherubinic Wanderer*, trans. Maria Shrady (Mahwah, New Jersey: Paulist Press, 1986), p. 49.
41. *The Wisdom of the Desert: Sayings from the Desert Fathers of the Fourth Century*, trans. Thomas Merton (New York: New Directions, 1960), p. 30.
42. *Ibid.*
43. *The Desert Fathers*, trans. Helen Waddell, (New York: Henry Holt and Co., 1936), pp. 92-93.
44. On the spirituality of the Quaker tradition see *Quaker Spirituality: Selected Writings*, ed. Douglas Steere, (New York: Paulist Press, 1984).

Poverty

45. Now at this time Caesar Augustus issued a decree for a census . . . (Luke 2:1-7).
46. *Ephrem the Syrian: Hymns*, trans. Kathleen E. McVey(New York: Paulist Press, 1989), pp. 82, 73-74, 106.
47. *Frances and Clare: The Complete Works* (New York: Paulist Press, 1982), p. 192.

God-With-Us

48. In the sixth month the angel Gabriel was sent . . . (Luke 1:26-38).
49. Guerric of Igny, *Liturgical Sermons*, Vol. 2, trans. Monks of Mount Saint Bernard Abbey (Spencer, Massachusetts: Cistercian Publications, 1971), pp. 44-45.
50. *Ibid.*, pp. 45-46.
51. *The Poems of Gerard Manley Hopkins*, 4th ed. (New York: Oxford University Press, 1967), pp. 93-97.
52. You see, God's grace has been revealed . . . (Titus 2:11-13).
53. This is an original and unpublished transalation from Philip Fischer.
54. Caryll Houselander, *The Reed of God* (Westminster, Maryland: Christian Classics, 1987), pp. 1 and 48.

55. St. Bonaventure, *Bringing Forth Christ: Five Feasts of the Child Jesus*, trans. Eric Doyle (Fairacres, Oxford, England: SLG Press), pp. 3-4.

56. Mary set out at that time and went as quickly as she could . . . (Luke 1:39-45).

57. Jeremy Taylor, *Selected Works*, ed. and intro. Thomas K. Carroll (Mahwah, New Jersey: Paulist Press, 1990), pp. 3-4.

LIVING THE SEASON

58. *Ephrem the Syrian: Hymns*, trans. Kathleen E. McVey (Mahawah, New Jersey: Paulist Press, 1989).

Dark

59. Technically the season ends the evening before the Feast of the Baptism (which falls right after Epiphany), but for all intents and purposes Epiphany is the culmination of Advent and Christmas. There are two other minor feasts associated with the season that are observed outside the liturgical boundaries of Advent-Epiphany. These are the Presentation (February 2) and the Annunciation (March 25). The former is a feast of lights and known popularly in England as *Candlemas*. It commemorates the presentation of the child Jesus in the temple of Jerusalem at the time prescribed in Mosaic Law for the new mother to be ritually purified after childbirth and a first born son to be consecrated to God. Simeon's canticle, the Nunc Dimittis, is sung and his prophecy that the child has come as a light to all nations is proclaimed. The latter feast falls within the Lenten cycle so that, at the moment when our attention is focused on the paschal mystery, we are alerted to the truth that within our dying is found the harbinger of new life.

60. When they heard this . . . they were infuriated . . . (Acts 7:54-60).

61. I am sending you like sheep among wolves . . . (Matthew 10:16-17, 22).

62. Herod was furious on realising he had been fooled . . . (Matthew 2:16-18).

63. Annie Dillard, *Teaching A Stone to Talk* (New York: Harper & Row 1988), p. 31.

Peace

64. In the countryside close by there were shepherds . . . (Luke 2:8-14).

65. On this topic cf. John R. Donahue, "The Good News of Peace" in *The Way*, p. 22 (1982).

66. God sent his word to the people of Israel . . . (Acts 10:36).

67. May Yahweh bless you and keep you . . . (Numbers 6:24-26).

68. His father Zechariah was filled with the Holy Spirit . . . (Luke 1:67-79).

69. Now, Master, you can let your servant go in peace . . . (Luke 2:29-32).

70. One booklet, *To Proclaim Peace: Religious Communities Speak Out on the Arm's Race*, ed. John Donaghy (Nyack, N.Y.: Fellowship Pub., 1983), contains statements about peace issued before 1983 by over twenty denominations. Since 1983, the United Methodist (1986), Presbyterian (1988), and Roman Catholic (1983) communities have each issued major statements on peace.

71. The Christian tradition of peacemaking is chronicled in Ronald G. Musto, *The Catholic Peace Tradition* (Maryknoll, New York: Orbis Books, 1986). See also Jaroslav Pelikan, *Jesus Through the Centuries* (New York: Harper and Row, 1985), especially pp. 168-181.

72. They will hammer their swords into ploughshares . . . (Isaiah 2:4).

73. Now when the angels had gone from them into heaven. . . (Luke 2:15-20).

74. Brother Lawrence, *The Practice of the Presence of God* (New York: Fleming Revell, 1958), p. 15.

75. You shall be called . . . (Luke 1:76-77).

Light

77. Arise, shine out, for your light has come . . . (Isaiah 60:1-6).

78. *The Apostolic Fathers, Vol. I*, Loeb Classical Library, trans. Kirsopp Lake (Cambridge, MA: Harvard University Press, 1970), p. 193.

79. As soon as Jesus was baptized he came up from the water . . . (Matthew 3:16-17).

80. Clement of Alexandria, *Exhortation to the Greeks 2*.

81. Jesus took with him Peter and James and his brother John and led them up a high mountain . . . (Matthew 17:1-8).

82. Gregory Palamas, *Triads* I, as quoted in John Meyendorff, *St. Gregory Palamas and Orthodox Spirituality*, trans. Adele Fiske (St. Vladimir's Seminary Press, 1974), p. 112.

83. *Choix de Sermons et Discours de E. Em. Mgr. Philarette*, trans. A. Serpinet, I, Paris, 1886, pp. 8-9, quoted in Meyendorff, *St. Gregory Palamas and Orthodox Spirituality*, pp. 127-29.

84. After Jesus had been born at Bethlehem in Judea . . . (Matthew 2:1-12).

About the Author

WENDY M. WRIGHT is recognized as one of the truly gifted writers in the field of contemporary spirituality. Her writings can be found in *Weavings* and other leading journals of the spiritual life as well as in her previously published books. She is on the faculty at Creighton University in Omaha, Nebraska, where she lives with her husband and three children. This is her first Upper Room Book.